MW00423301

Rule Book of Games
Volleyball

Vance Hawkins

Alpha Editions

Copyright © 2018

ISBN : 9789352976911

Design and Setting By
Alpha Editions
email - alphaedis@gmail.com

All rights reserved. No part of this publication may be reproduced, distributed, or transmitted in any form or by means, including photocopying, recording, or other electronic or mechanical methods, without the prior written permission of the publisher.

The views and characters expressed in the book are of the author and his/her imagination and do not represent the views of the Publisher.

Contents

Preface

Volleyball is a team sport in which two teams of six players are separated by a net. Each team tries to score points by grounding a ball on the other team's court under organized rules. It has been a part of the official program of the Summer Olympic Games since 1964.

The game of volleyball is a dandy game and more besides. At its top level competitive aspect, it is a fast moving energetic game demanding skill, strength, agility, team work and intelligence from its players. At its lowest level, it is an enjoyable, easily set-up game from which youngsters and beginners of all ages can quickly gain pleasure and satisfaction.

Volleyball is a team game which can be played indoors as well as outdoors. On the playing court this game is played which is divided by a net. The object of the game is to send the ball over a net in order to ground it on the opponent's court, and to prevent the same effort by the opponent.

The complete rules are extensive, but simply, play proceeds as follows: a player on one of the teams begins a 'rally' by serving the ball (tossing or releasing it and then hitting it with a hand or arm), from behind the back boundary line of the court, over the net, and into the receiving team's court. The receiving team must not let the ball be grounded within their court. The team may touch the ball up to 3 times but individual players may not touch the ball twice consecutively. Typically, the first two touches are used to set up for an attack, an attempt to direct the ball back over the net in such a way that the serving team is unable to prevent it from being grounded in their court.

Volleyball is essentially a game of transition from one of the above skills to the next, with choreographed team movement between plays on the ball. These team movements are determined by the teams chosen serve receive system, offensive system, coverage system, and defensive system. The serve receive system is the formation used by the receiving team to attempt to pass the ball to the designated setter. Systems can consist of 5 receivers, 4 receivers, 3 receivers, and in some cases 2 receivers. The most popular formation at higher levels is a 3 receiver formation consisting of two left sides and a libero receiving every rotation. This allows middles and right sides to become more specialized at hitting and blocking.

A volleyball court is 30 feet wide and 60 feet long; each side of the net is 30 feet by 30 feet. A 2-inch line borders the court to serve as the out-of-bounds line. Any ball that touches the line during play is still considered "in" the court. In volleyball, there are six people on the court at one time for each team. Usually three people are in the front row, and three are in the back row. The front row is sectioned off by a line 10 feet from the net, called the "attack line" or the "10-foot line." Front-row players are not confined to this section of the court, but this is where most of their playing takes place.

This is a reference book. All the matter is just compiled and edited in nature, taken from the various sources which are in public domain.

It is hoped that this book will help the sportsperson, professors, readers, coaches, instructors, students of physical education and for the general readers too.

—Editor

1

An Introduction

Volleyball is a team sport in which two teams of six players are separated by a net. Each team tries to score points by grounding a ball on the other team's court under organized rules. It has been a part of the official program of the Summer Olympic Games since 1964.

The complete rules are extensive, but simply, play proceeds as follows: a player on one of the teams begins a 'rally' by serving the ball (tossing or releasing it and then hitting it with a hand or arm), from behind the back boundary line of the court, over the net, and into the receiving team's court. The receiving team must not let the ball be grounded within their court. The team may touch the ball up to 3 times but individual players may not touch the ball twice consecutively. Typically, the first two touches are used to set up for an attack, an attempt to direct the ball back over the net in such a way that the serving team is unable to prevent it from being grounded in their court.

The rally continues, with each team allowed as many as three consecutive touches, until either (1): a team makes a *kill*, grounding the ball on the opponent's court and winning the rally; or (2): a team commits a *fault* and loses the rally. The team that wins the rally is awarded a point, and serves the ball to start the next rally. A few of the most common faults include:

- causing the ball to touch the ground or floor outside the opponents' court or without first passing over the net;

- *catching and throwing* the ball;
- *double hit*: two consecutive contacts with the ball made by the same player;
- four consecutive contacts with the ball made by the same team;
- net foul: touching the net during play;
- foot fault: the foot crosses over the boundary line when serving.

The ball is usually played with the hands or arms, but players can legally strike or push (short contact) the ball with any part of the body.

A number of consistent techniques have evolved in volleyball, including *spiking* and *blocking* (because these plays are made above the top of the net, the vertical jump is an athletic skill emphasized in the sport) as well as *passing*, *setting*, and specialized player positions and offensive and defensive structures.

HISTORY

Origin of volleyball

On February 9, 1895, in Holyoke, Massachusetts (United States), William G. Morgan, a YMCA physical education director, created a new game called *Mintonette*, a name derived from the game of badminton, as a pastime to be played (preferably) indoors and by any number of players.

The game took some of its characteristics from tennis and handball.

Another indoor sport, basketball, was catching on in the area, having been invented just ten miles (sixteen kilometers) away in the city of Springfield, Massachusetts, only four years before.

Mintonette was designed to be an indoor sport, less rough than basketball, for older members of the YMCA, while still requiring a bit of athletic effort.

The first rules, written down by William G Morgan, called for a net 6 ft 6 in (1.98 m) high, a 25 ft × 50 ft (7.6 m × 15.2 m) court, and any number of players.

A match was composed of nine innings with three serves for each team in each inning, and no limit to the number of ball contacts for each team before sending the ball to the opponents' court.

In case of a serving error, a second try was allowed. Hitting the ball into the net was considered a foul (with loss of the point or a side-out)—except in the case of the first-try serve.

After an observer, Alfred Halstead, noticed the volleying nature of the game at its first exhibition match in 1896, played at the International YMCA Training School (now called Springfield College), the game quickly became known as *volleyball* (it was originally spelled as two words: "*volley ball*"). Volleyball rules were slightly modified by the International YMCA Training School and the game spread around the country to various YMCAs.

A scene of playing Volleyball of the village Naldahari in India

Refinements and later developments

The first official ball used in volleyball is disputed; some sources say that Spalding created the first official ball in 1896, while others claim it was created in 1900. The rules evolved over time: in the Philippines by 1916, the skill and power of the set and spike had been introduced, and four years later a "three hits" rule and a rule against hitting from the back row were established. In 1917, the game was changed from 21 to 15 points.

In 1919, about 16,000 volleyballs were distributed by the American Expeditionary Forces to their troops and allies, which sparked the growth of volleyball in new countries.

Japanese American women playing volleyball, Manzanar internment camp, California, ca. 1943

The first country outside the United States to adopt volleyball was Canada in 1900. An international federation, the Fédération Internationale de Volleyball (FIVB), was founded in 1947, and the first World Championships were held in 1949 for men and 1952 for women.

The sport is now popular in Brazil, in Europe (where especially Italy, the Netherlands, and countries from Eastern Europe have been major forces since the late 1980s), in Russia, and in other countries including China and the rest of Asia, as well as in the United States.

A nudist/naturist volleyball game at the Sunny Trails Club during the 1958 Canadian Sunbathing Association (CSA) convention in British Columbia, Canada

Beach volleyball, a variation of the game played on sand and with only two players per team, became a FIVB-endorsed variation in 1987 and was added to the Olympic program at the 1996 Summer Olympics.

Volleyball is also a sport at the Paralympics managed by the World Organization Volleyball for Disabled.

Nudists were early adopters of the game with regular organized play in clubs as early as the late 1920s. By the 1960s, a volleyball court had become standard in almost all nudist/naturist clubs.

Volleyball in the Olympics

Volleyball has been part of the Summer Olympics program for both men and women consistently since 1964.

RULES OF THE GAME

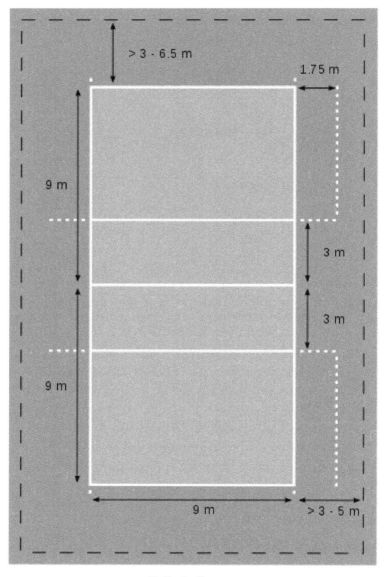

Volleyball court

The court dimensions

A volleyball court is 9 m × 18 m (29.5 ft × 59.1 ft), divided into equal square halves by a net with a width of one meter (39.4 in). The top of the net is 2.43 m (7 ft 11 D_{16} in) above the center of the court for men's competition, and 2.24 m (7 ft 4 D_{16} in) for women's competition, varied for veterans and junior competitions.

The minimum height clearance for indoor volleyball courts is 7 m (23.0 ft), although a clearance of 8 m (26.2 ft) is recommended.

A line 3 m (9.8 ft) from and parallel to the net is considered the "attack line". This "3 meter" (or "10-foot") line divides the court into "back row" and "front row" areas (also back court and front court). These are in turn divided into 3 areas each: these are numbered as follows, starting from area "1", which is the position of the serving player:

After a team gains the serve (also known as siding out), its members must rotate in a clockwise direction, with the player previously in area "2" moving to area "1" and so on, with the player from area "1" moving to area "6". Each player rotates only one time after the team gains possession of the serve; the next time each player rotates will be after the other team wins possession of the ball and loses the point.

The team courts are surrounded by an area called the free zone which is a minimum of 3 meters wide and which the players may enter and play within after the service of the ball. All lines denoting the boundaries of the team court and the attack zone are drawn or painted within the dimensions of the area and are therefore a part of the court or zone. If a ball comes in contact with the line, the ball is considered to be "in". An antenna is placed on each side of the net perpendicular to the sideline and is a vertical extension of the side boundary of the court. A ball passing over the net must pass completely between the antennae (or their theoretical extensions to the ceiling) without contacting them.

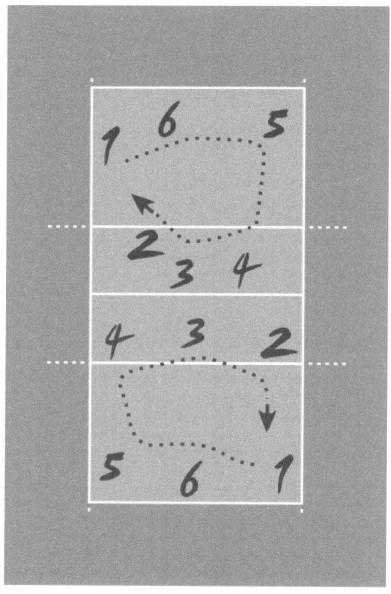

Rotation pattern

The ball

FIVB regulations state that the ball must be spherical, made of leather or synthetic leather, have a circumference of 65–67 cm, a weight of 260–280 g and an inside pressure of 0.30–0.325 kg/cm. Other governing bodies have similar regulations.

Game play

White is on the attack while red attempts to block.

Buddhist monks play volleyball in the Himalayan state of Sikkim, India.

Each team consists of six players. To get play started, a team is chosen to serve by coin toss. A player from the serving team throws the ball into the air and attempts to hit the ball so it passes over the net on a course such that it will land in the opposing team's court (the *serve*). The opposing team must use a combination of no more than three contacts with the volleyball to return the ball to the opponent's side of the net. These contacts usually consist first of the *bump* or *pass* so that the ball's trajectory is aimed towards the player designated as the *setter*; second of the *set* (usually an over-hand pass using wrists to push finger-tips at the ball) by the setter so that the ball's trajectory is aimed towards a spot where one of the players designated as an *attacker* can hit it, and third by the *attacker* who *spikes* (jumping, raising one arm above the head and hitting the ball so it will move quickly down to the ground on the opponent's court) to return the ball over the net. The team with possession of the ball that is trying to attack the ball as described is said to be on *offense.*

The team on *defense* attempts to prevent the attacker from directing the ball into their court: players at the net jump and reach above the top (and if possible, across the plane) of the net to *block* the attacked ball. If the ball is hit around, above, or through the block, the defensive players arranged in the rest of the court attempt to control the ball with a *dig* (usually a forearm pass of a hard-driven ball). After a successful dig, the team transitions to offense.

The game continues in this manner, rallying back and forth, until the ball touches the court within the boundaries or until an error is made.

The most frequent errors that are made are either to fail to return the ball over the net within the allowed three touches, or to cause the ball to land outside the court. A ball is "in" if any part of it touches a sideline or end-line, and a strong spike may compress the ball enough when it lands that a ball which at first appears to be going out may actually be in. Players may travel well outside the court to play a ball that has gone over a sideline or end-line in the air.

Other common errors include a player touching the ball twice in succession, a player "catching" the ball, a player touching the net while attempting to play the ball, or a player penetrating under the net into the opponent's court. There are a large number of other errors specified in the rules, although most of them are infrequent occurrences.

These errors include back-row or libero players spiking the ball or blocking (back-row players may spike the ball if they jump from behind the attack line), players not being in the correct position when the ball is served, attacking the serve in the front court and above the height of the net, using another player as a source of support to reach the ball, stepping over the back boundary line when serving, taking more than 8 seconds to serve, or playing the ball when it is above the opponent's court.

Scoring

Scorer's table just before a game

When the ball contacts the floor within the court boundaries or an error is made, the team that did not make the error is awarded a point, whether they served the ball or not. If the ball hits the line, the ball is counted as in.

The team that won the point serves for the next point. If the team that won the point served in the previous point, the same player serves again. If the team that won the point did not serve the previous point, the players of the serving team rotate their position on the court in a clockwise manner. The game continues, with the first team to score 25 points by a two-point margin awarded the set. Matches are best-of-five sets and the fifth set, if necessary, is usually played to 15 points. (Scoring differs between leagues, tournaments, and levels; high schools sometimes play best-of-three to 25; in the NCAAmatches are played best-of-five to 25 as of the 2008 season.)

Before 1999, points could be scored only when a team had the serve (*side-out scoring*) and all sets went up to only 15 points.

The FIVB changed the rules in 1999 (with the changes being compulsory in 2000) to use the current scoring system (formerly known as *rally point system*), primarily to make the length of the match more predictable and to make the game more spectator- and television-friendly.

The final year of side-out scoring at the NCAA Division I Women's Volleyball Championship was 2000. Rally point scoring debuted in 2001, and games were played to 30 points through 2007. For the 2008 season, games were renamed "sets" and reduced to 25 points to win. Most high schools in the U.S. changed to rally scoring in 2003, and several states implemented it the previous year on an experimental basis.

Libero

The libero player was introduced internationally in 1998, and made its debut for NCAA competition in 2002. The libero is a player specialized in defensive skills: the libero must wear a contrasting jersey color from his or her teammates and cannot block or attack the ball when it is entirely above net height.

When the ball is not in play, the libero can replace any back-row player, without prior notice to the officials. This replacement does not count against the substitution limit each team is allowed per set, although the libero may be replaced only by the player whom he or she replaced. Most U.S. high schools added the libero position from 2003 to 2005.

The libero may function as a setter only under certain restrictions. If she/he makes an overhand set, she/he must be standing behind (and not stepping on) the 3-meter line; otherwise, the ball cannot be attacked above the net in front of the 3-meter line. An underhand pass is allowed from any part of the court.

The libero is, generally, the most skilled defensive player on the team. There is also a libero tracking sheet, where the referees or officiating team must keep track of whom the libero subs in and out for. There may only be one libero per set (game), although there may be a different libero in the beginning of any new set (game).

Furthermore, a libero is not allowed to serve, according to international rules, with the exception of the NCAA women's volleyball games, where a 2004 rule change allows the libero to serve, but only in a specific rotation. That is, the libero can only serve for one person, not for all of the people for whom she goes in. That rule change was also applied to high school and junior high play soon after.

Recent rule changes

Other rule changes enacted in 2000 include allowing serves in which the ball touches the net, as long as it goes over the net into the opponents' court.

Also, the service area was expanded to allow players to serve from anywhere behind the end line but still within the theoretical extension of the sidelines. Other changes were made to lighten up calls on faults for carries and double-touches, such as allowing multiple contacts by a single player ("double-hits") on a team's first contact provided that they are a part of a single play on the ball.

In 2008, the NCAA changed the minimum number of points needed to win any of the first four sets from 30 to 25 for women's volleyball (men's volleyball remained at 30.) If a fifth (deciding) set is reached, the minimum required score remains at 15. In addition, the word "game" is now referred to as "set".

Changes in rules have been studied and announced by the FIVB in recent years, and they have released the updated rules in 2009.

SKILLS

Competitive teams master six basic skills: serve, pass, set, attack, block and dig. Each of these skills comprises a number of specific techniques that have been introduced over the years and are now considered standard practice in high-level volleyball.

Serve

A player making a jump serve

3D animation floating serve

A player stands behind the inline and serves the ball, in an attempt to drive it into the opponent's court. The main objective is to make it land inside the court; it is also desirable to set the ball's direction, speed and acceleration so that it becomes difficult for the receiver to handle it properly. A serve is called an "ace" when the ball lands directly onto the court or travels outside the court after being touched by an opponent.

In contemporary volleyball, many types of serves are employed:

- Underhand: a serve in which the player strikes the ball below the waist instead of tossing it up and striking it with an overhand throwing motion. Underhand serves are considered very easy to receive and are rarely employed in high-level competitions.

- Sky ball serve: a specific type of underhand serve occasionally used in beach volleyball, where the ball is hit so high it comes down almost in a straight line. This serve was invented and employed almost exclusively by the Brazilian team in the early 1980s and is now considered outdated. During the 2016 Olympic Games in Rio de Janeiro, however, the sky ball serve was extensively played by Italian beach volleyball player Adrian Carambula. In Brazil, this serve is called *Jornada nas Estrelas* (Star Trek)

- Topspin: an overhand serve where the player tosses the ball high and hits it with a wrist snap, giving it topspin which causes it to drop faster than it would otherwise and helps maintain a straight flight path. Topspin serves are generally hit hard and aimed at a specific returner or part of the court. Standing topspin serves are rarely used above the high school level of play.

- Float: an overhand serve where the ball is hit with no spin so that its path becomes unpredictable, akin to a knuckleball in baseball.

- Jump serve: an overhand serve where the ball is first tossed high in the air, then the player makes a timed approach and jumps to make contact with the ball, hitting it with much pace and topspin. This is the most popular serve amongst college and professional teams.

- Jump float: an overhand serve where the ball is tossed high enough that the player may jump before hitting it similarly to a standing float serve. The ball is tossed lower than a topspin jump serve, but contact is still made while in the air. This serve is becoming more popular amongst college and professional players because it has a certain unpredictability in its flight pattern. It is the only serve where the server's feet can go over the inline.

Pass

A player making a forearm pass or bump

Also called reception, the pass is the attempt by a team to properly handle the opponent's serve, or any form of attack. Proper handling includes not only preventing the ball from touching the court, but also making it reach the position where the setter is standing quickly and precisely.

The skill of passing involves fundamentally two specific techniques: underarm pass, or bump, where the ball touches the inside part of the joined forearms or platform, at waist line; and overhand pass, where it is handled with the fingertips, like a set, above the head.

Either are acceptable in professional and beach volleyball; however, there are much tighter regulations on the overhand pass in beach volleyball.

Set

The set is usually the second contact that a team makes with the ball. The main goal of setting is to put the ball in the air in such a way that it can be driven by an attack into the opponent's court. The setter coordinates the offensive movements of a team, and is the player who ultimately decides which player will actually attack the ball.

Jump set

As with passing, one may distinguish between an overhand and a bump set. Since the former allows for more control over the speed and direction of the ball, the bump is used only when the ball is so low it cannot be properly handled with fingertips, or in beach volleyball where rules regulating overhand setting are more stringent. In the case of a set, one also speaks of a front or back set, meaning whether the ball is passed in the direction the setter is facing or behind the setter. There is also a jump set that is used when the ball is too close to the net. In this case the setter usually jumps off his or her right foot straight up to avoid going into the net. The setter usually stands about T! of the way from the left to the right of the net and faces the left.

Sometimes a setter refrains from raising the ball for a teammate to perform an attack and tries to play it directly onto the opponent's court. This movement is called a "dump". This can only be performed when the setter is in the front row, otherwise it constitutes an illegal back court attack. The most common dumps are to 'throw' the ball behind the setter or in front of the setter to zones 2 and 4. More experienced setters toss the ball into the deep corners or spike the ball on the second hit.

As with a set or an overhand pass, the setter/passer must be careful to touch the ball with both hands at the same time. If one hand is noticeably late to touch the ball this could result in a less effective set, as well as the referee calling a 'double hit' and giving the point to the opposing team.

Attack

A Spanish player, #18 in red outfit, about to spike towards the Portuguesefield, whose players try to block the way

The attack, also known as the *spike*, is usually the third contact a team makes with the ball. The object of attacking is to handle the ball so that it lands on the opponent's court and cannot be defended. A player makes a series of steps (the "approach"), jumps, and swings at the ball.

Ideally the contact with the ball is made at the apex of the hitter's jump. At the moment of contact, the hitter's arm is fully extended above his or her head and slightly forward, making the highest possible contact while maintaining the ability to deliver a powerful hit. The hitter uses arm swing, wrist snap, and a rapid forward contraction of the entire body to drive the ball. A 'bounce' is a slang term for a very hard/loud spike that follows an almost straight trajectory steeply downward into the opponent's court and bounces very high into the air. A "kill" is the slang term for an attack that is not returned by the other team thus resulting in a point.

Contemporary volleyball comprises a number of attacking techniques:

- Backcourt (or backrow)/pipe attack: an attack performed by a back row player. The player must jump from behind the 3-meter line before making contact with the ball, but may land in front of the 3-meter line.

- Line and Cross-court Shot: refers to whether the ball flies in a straight trajectory parallel to the side lines, or crosses through the court in an angle. A cross-court shot with a very pronounced angle, resulting in the ball landing near the 3-meter line, is called a cut shot.

- Dip/Dink/Tip/Cheat/Dump: the player does not try to make a hit, but touches the ball lightly, so that it lands on an area of the opponent's court that is not being covered by the defense.

- Tool/Wipe/Block-abuse: the player does not try to make a hard spike, but hits the ball so that it touches the opponent's block and then bounces off-court.

- Off-speed hit: the player does not hit the ball hard, reducing its speed and thus confusing the opponent's defense.

- Quick hit/"One": an attack (usually by the middle blocker) where the approach and jump begin before the setter contacts the ball. The set (called a "quick set") is placed only slightly above the net and the ball is struck by the hitter almost immediately after leaving the setter's hands. Quick attacks are often effective because they isolate the middle blocker to be the only blocker on the hit.

- Slide: a variation of the quick hit that uses a low back set. The middle hitter steps around the setter and hits from behind him or her.

- Double quick hit/"Stack"/"Tandem": a variation of quick hit where two hitters, one in front and one behind the setter or both in front of the setter, jump to perform a quick hit at the same time. It can be used to deceive opposite blockers and free a fourth hitter attacking from back-court, maybe without block at all.

Block

Three players performing a block

Blocking refers to the actions taken by players standing at the net to stop or alter an opponent's attack.

A block that is aimed at completely stopping an attack, thus making the ball remain in the opponent's court, is called offensive. A well-executed offensive block is performed by jumping and reaching to penetrate with one's arms and hands over the net and into the opponent's area. It requires anticipating the direction the ball will go once the attack takes place. It may also require calculating the best foot work to executing the "perfect" block.

The jump should be timed so as to intercept the ball's trajectory prior to it crossing over the net. Palms are held deflected downward about 45–60 degrees toward the interior of the opponents court. A "roof" is a spectacular offensive block that redirects the power and speed of the attack straight down to the attacker's floor, as if the attacker hit the ball into the underside of a peaked house roof.

By contrast, it is called a defensive, or "soft" block if the goal is to control and deflect the hard-driven ball up so that it slows down and becomes easier to defend. A well-executed soft-block is performed by jumping and placing one's hands above the net with no penetration into the opponent's court and with the palms up and fingers pointing backward.

Blocking is also classified according to the number of players involved. Thus, one may speak of single (or solo), double, or triple block.

Successful blocking does not always result in a "roof" and many times does not even touch the ball. While it's obvious that a block was a success when the attacker is roofed, a block that consistently forces the attacker away from his or her 'power' or preferred attack into a more easily controlled shot by the defense is also a highly successful block.

At the same time, the block position influences the positions where other defenders place themselves while opponent hitters are spiking.

Dig

Player going for a dig

Digging is the ability to prevent the ball from touching one's court after a spike or attack, particularly a ball that is nearly touching the ground. In many aspects, this skill is similar to passing, or bumping: overhand dig and bump are also used to distinguish between defensive actions taken with fingertips or with joined arms. It varies from passing however in that is it a much more reflex based skill, especially at the higher levels.

It is especially important while digging for players to stay on their toes; several players choose to employ a split step to make sure they're ready to move in any direction.

Some specific techniques are more common in digging than in passing. A player may sometimes perform a "dive", i.e., throw his or her body in the air with a forward movement in an attempt to save the ball, and land on his or her chest. When the player also slides his or her hand under a ball that is almost touching the court, this is called a "pancake". The pancake is frequently used in indoor volleyball, but rarely if ever in beach volleyball because the uneven and yielding nature of the sand court limits the chances that the ball will make a good, clean contact with the hand. When used correctly, it is one of the more spectacular defensive volleyball plays.

Sometimes a player may also be forced to drop his or her body quickly to the floor to save the ball. In this situation, the player makes use of a specific rolling technique to minimize the chances of injuries.

TEAM PLAY

U.S. women's team doing team planning

Volleyball is essentially a game of transition from one of the above skills to the next, with choreographed team movement between plays on the ball. These team movements are determined by the teams chosen serve receive system, offensive system, coverage system, and defensive system.

The serve receive system is the formation used by the receiving team to attempt to pass the ball to the designated setter. Systems can consist of 5 receivers, 4 receivers, 3 receivers, and in some cases 2 receivers. The most popular formation at higher levels is a 3 receiver formation consisting of two left sides and a libero receiving every rotation. This allows middles and right sides to become more specialized at hitting and blocking.

Offensive systems are the formations used by the offense to attempt to ground the ball into the opposing court (or otherwise score points). Formations often include designated player positions with skill specialization. Popular formations include the 4-2, 6-2, and 5-1 systems. There are also several different attacking schemes teams can use to keep the opposing defense off balance.

Young women on the court

Coverage systems are the formations used by the offense to protect their court in the case of a blocked attack. Executed by the 5 offensive players not directly attacking the ball, players move to assigned positions around the attacker to dig up any ball that deflects off the block back into their own court. Popular formations include the 2-3 system and the 1-2-2 system. In lieu of a system, some teams just use a random coverage with the players nearest the hitter.

Defensive systems are the formations used by the defense to protect against the ball being grounded into their court by the opposing team. The system will outline which players are responsible for which areas of the court depending on where the opposing team is attacking from. Popular systems include the 6-Up, 6-Back-Deep, and 6-Back-Slide defense. There are also several different blocking schemes teams can employ to disrupt the opposing teams offense.

Some teams, when they are ready to serve, will line up their other five players in a screen to obscure the view of the receiving team. This action is only illegal if the server makes use of the screen, so the call is made at the referees discretion as to the impact the screen made on the receivers ability to pass the ball. The most common style of screening involves a W formation designed to take up as much horizontal space as possible.

COACHING

Basic

Coaching for volleyball can be classified under two main categories: match coaching and developmental coaching. The objective of match coaching is to win a match by managing a team's strategy. Developmental coaching emphasizes player development through the reinforcement of basic skills during exercises known as "drills." Drills promote repetition and refinement of volleyball movements, particularly in footwork patterns, body positioning relative to others, and ball contact. A coach will construct drills that simulate match situations thereby encouraging speed of movement, anticipation, timing, communication, and team-work. At the various stages of a player's career, a coach will tailor drills to meet the strategic requirements of the team. The American Volleyball Coaches Association is the largest organization in the world dedicated exclusively to volleyball coaching.

STRATEGY

An image from an international match between Italy and Russia in 2005. A Russian player on the left has just served, with three men of his team next to the net moving to their assigned block positions from the starting ones. Two others, in the back-row positions, are preparing for defense. Italy, on the right, has three men in a line, each preparing to pass if the ball reaches him. The setter is waiting for their pass while the middle hitter with no. 10 will jump for a quick hit if the pass is good enough. Alessandro Fei (no. 14) has no passing duties and is preparing for a back-row hit on the right side of the field. Note the two liberos with different color dress. Middle hitters/blockers are commonly substituted by liberos in their back-row positions.

Player specialization

There are 5 positions filled on every volleyball team at the elite level. Setter, Outside Hitter/Left Side Hitter, Middle Hitter, Opposite Hitter/Right Side Hitter and Libero/Defensive Specialist. Each of these positions plays a specific, key role in winning a volleyball match.

- Setters have the task for orchestrating the offense of the team. They aim for second touch and their main responsibility is to place the ball in the air where the attackers can place the ball into the opponents' court for a point. They have to be able to operate with the hitters, manage the tempo of their side of the court and choose the right attackers to set. Setters need to have swift and skillful appraisal and tactical accuracy, and must be quick at moving around the court.

• Liberos are defensive players who are responsible for receiving the attack or serve. They are usually the players on the court with the quickest reaction time and best passing skills. *Libero* means 'free' in Italian – they receive this name as they have the ability to substitute for any other player on the court during each play. They do not necessarily need to be tall, as they never play at the net, which allows shorter players with strong passing and defensive skills to excel in the position and play an important role in the team's success. A player designated as a libero for a match may not play other roles during that match. Liberos wear a different color jersey than their teammates.

• Middle blockers or Middle hitters are players that can perform very fast attacks that usually take place near the setter. They are specialized in blocking, since they must attempt to stop equally fast plays from their opponents and then quickly set up a double block at the sides of the court. In non-beginners play, every team will have two middle hitters.

• Outside hitters or Left side hitters attack from near the left antenna. The outside hitter is usually the most consistent hitter on the team and gets the most sets. Inaccurate first passes usually result in a set to the outside hitter rather than middle or opposite. Since most sets to the outside are high, the outside hitter may take a longer approach, always starting from outside the court sideline. In non-beginners play, there are again two outside hitters on every team in every match.

• Opposite hitters or Right-side hitters carry the defensive workload for a volleyball team in the front row. Their primary responsibilities are to put up a well formed block against the opponents' *Outside Hitters* and serve as a backup setter. Sets to the opposite usually go to the right side of the antennae.

At some levels where substitutions are unlimited, teams will make use of a Defensive Specialist in place of or in addition to a Libero. This position does not have unique rules like the libero position, instead, these players are used to substitute out a poor back row defender using regular substitution rules. A defensive specialist is often used if you have a particularly poor back court defender in right side or left side, but your team is already using a libero to take out your middles. Most often, the situation involves a team using a right side player with a big block who must be subbed out in the back row because they aren't able to effectively play back court defense. Similarly, teams might use a Serving Specialist to sub out a poor server situationally.

Formations

The three standard volleyball formations are known as "4–2", "6–2" and "5–1", which refers to the number of hitters and setters respectively. 4–2 is a basic formation used only in beginners' play, while 5–1 is by far the most common formation in high-level play.

4–2

The 4–2 formation has four hitters and two setters. The setters usually set from the middle front or right front position. The team will therefore have two front-row attackers at all times. In the international 4–2, the setters set from the right front position. The international 4–2 translates more easily into other forms of offense.

The setters line up opposite each other in the rotation. The typical lineup has two outside hitters. By aligning like positions opposite themselves in the rotation, there will always be one of each position in the front and back rows. After service, the players in the front row move into their assigned positions, so that the setter is always in middle front. Alternatively, the setter moves into the right front and has both a middle and an outside attacker; the disadvantage here lies in the lack of an offside hitter, allowing one of the other team's blockers to "cheat in" on a middle block.

The clear disadvantage to this offensive formation is that there are only two attackers, leaving a team with fewer offensive weapons.

Another aspect is to see the setter as an attacking force, albeit a weakened force, because when the setter is in the front court they are able to 'tip' or 'dump', so when the ball is close to the net on the second touch, the setter may opt to hit the ball over with one hand. This means that the blocker who would otherwise not have to block the setter is engaged and may allow one of the hitters to have an easier attack.

6–2

In the 6–2 formation, a player always comes forward from the back row to set. The three front row players are all in attacking positions. Thus, all six players act as hitters at one time or another, while two can act as setters. So the 6–2 formation is actually a 4–2 system, but the back-row setter penetrates to set.

The 6–2 lineup thus requires two setters, who line up opposite to each other in the rotation. In addition to the setters, a typical lineup will have two middle hitters and two outside hitters. By aligning like positions opposite themselves in the rotation, there will always be one of each position in the front and back rows. After service, the players in the front row move into their assigned positions.

The advantage of the 6–2 is that there are always three front-row hitters available, maximizing the offensive possibilities. However, not only does the 6–2 require a team to possess two people capable of performing the highly specialized role of setter, it also requires both of those players to be effective offensive hitters when not in the setter position. At the international level, only the Cuban National Women's Team employs this kind of formation. It is also used by NCAA teams in Division III men's play and women's play in all divisions, partially due to the variant rules used which allow more substitutions per set than the 6 allowed in the standard rules—12 in matches involving two Division III men's teams and 15 for all women's play.

5–1

The 5–1 formation has only one player who assumes setting responsibilities regardless of his or her position in the rotation. The team will therefore have three front-row attackers when the setter is in the back row, and only two when the setter is in the front row, for a total of five possible attackers.

The player opposite the setter in a 5–1 rotation is called the *opposite hitter*. In general, opposite hitters do not pass; they stand behind their teammates when the opponent is serving. The opposite hitter may be used as a third attack option (back-row attack) when the setter is in the front row: this is the normal option used to increase the attack capabilities of modern volleyball teams.

Normally the opposite hitter is the most technically skilled hitter of the team. Back-row attacks generally come from the back-right position, known as zone 1, but are increasingly performed from back-center in high-level play.

The big advantage of this system is that the setter always has 3 hitters to vary sets with. If the setter does this well, the opponent's middle blocker may not have enough time to block with the outside blocker, increasing the chance for the attacking team to make a point.

There is another advantage, the same as that of a 4–2 formation: when the setter is a front-row player, he or she is allowed to jump and "dump" the ball onto the opponent's side. This too can confuse the opponent's blocking players: the setter can jump and dump or can set to one of the hitters. A good setter knows this and thus won't only jump to dump or to set for a quick hit, but when setting outside as well to confuse the opponent.

The 5–1 offense is actually a mix of 6–2 and 4–2: when the setter is in the front row, the offense looks like a 4–2; when the setter is in the back row, the offense looks like a 6–2.

VARIATIONS AND RELATED GAMES

There are many variations on the basic rules of volleyball. By far the most popular of these is beach volleyball, which is played on sand with two people per team, and rivals the main sport in popularity.

Some games related to volleyball include:

- Beachball volleyball: A game of indoor volleyball played with a beach ball instead of a volleyball.
- Biribol: an aquatic variant, played in shallow swimming pools. The name comes from the Brazilian city where it was invented, Birigui. Similar to Water volleyball.
- Ecua-volley: A variant invented in Ecuador, with some significant variants, such as number of players, and a heavier ball.
- Footvolley: A sport from Brazil in which the hands and arms are not used but most else is like beach volleyball.
- Hooverball: Popularized by President Herbert Hoover, it is played with a volleyball net and a medicine ball; it is scored like tennis, but the ball is caught and then thrown back. The weight of the medicine ball can make the sport quite physically demanding; annual championship tournaments are held annually in West Branch, Iowa.
- Newcomb ball (sometimes spelled "Nuke 'Em"): In this game, the ball is caught and thrown instead of hit; it rivaled volleyball in popularity until the 1920s.
- Prisoner Ball: Also played with volleyball court and a volleyball, prisoner ball is a variation of Newcomb ball where players are "taken prisoner" or released from "prison" instead of scoring points. Usually played by young children.

- Sepak Takraw: Played in Southeast Asia using a rattan ball and allowing only players' feet, knees, chest, and head to touch the ball.
- Snow volleyball: a variant of beach volleyball that is played on snow. The Fédération Internationale de Volleyball has announced its plans to make snow volleyball part of the future Winter Olympic Games programme.
- Throwball: became popular with women players at the YMCA College of Physical Education in Chennai (India) in the 1940s.
- Towel volleyball: towel volleyball is a popular entertainment outdoors. The game takes place in volleyball court, forming pairs that hold towels in their hands and try to throw the ball into the opponent's field. You can also play with blankets, held by four people. There may be some variations.
- Wallyball: A variation of volleyball played in a racquetball court with a rubber ball.

2

Historical Background of V olleyball

Volleyball, game played by two teams, usually of six players on a side, in which the players use their hands to bat a ball back and forth over a high net, trying to make the ball touch the court within the opponents' playing area before it can be returned.

Gilberto Godoy Filho of Brazil serving the ball at an indoor volleyball match in 2006.

To prevent this a player on the opposing team bats the ball up and toward a teammate before it touches the court surface— that teammate may then volley it back across the net or bat it to a third teammate who volleys it across the net. A team is allowed only three touches of the ball before it must be returned over the net.

History

Volleyball was invented in 1895 by William G. Morgan, physical director of the Young Men's Christian Association (YMCA) in Holyoke, Massachusetts. It was designed as an indoor sport for businessmen who found the new game of basketball too vigorous. Morgan called the sport "mintonette," until a professor from Springfield College in Massachusetts noted the volleying nature of play and proposed the name of "volleyball." The original rules were written by Morgan and printed in the first edition of the *Official Handbook of the Athletic League of the Young Men's Christian Associations of North America* (1897). The game soon proved to have wide appeal for both sexes in schools, playgrounds, the armed forces, and other organizations in the United States, and it was subsequently introduced to other countries.

In 1916 rules were issued jointly by the YMCA and the National Collegiate Athletic Association (NCAA). The first nationwide tournament in the United States was conducted by the National YMCA Physical Education Committee in New York City in 1922.

The United States Volleyball Association (USVBA) was formed in 1928 and recognized as the rules-making, governing body in the United States. From 1928 the USVBA—now known as USA Volleyball (USAV)—has conducted annual national men's and senior men's (age 35 and older) volleyball championships, except during 1944 and 1945. Its women's division was started in 1949, and a senior women's division (age 30 and older) was added in 1977. Other national events in the United States are conducted by member groups of the USAV such as the YMCA and the NCAA.

Volleyball was introduced into Europe by American troops during World War I, when national organizations were formed. The Fédération Internationale de Volley Ball (FIVB) was organized in Paris in 1947 and moved to Lausanne, Switzerland, in 1984. The USVBA was one of the 13 charter members of the FIVB, whose membership grew to more than 210 member countries by the late 20th century.

International volleyball competition began in 1913 with the first Far East Games, in Manila. During the early 1900s and continuing until after World War II, volleyball in Asia was played on a larger court, with a lower net, and nine players on a team.

The FIVB-sponsored world volleyball championships (for men only in 1949; for both men and women in 1952 and succeeding years) led to acceptance of standardized playing rules and officiating. Volleyball became an Olympic sport for both men and women at the 1964 Olympic Games in Tokyo.

European championships were long dominated by Czechoslovakian, Hungarian, Polish, Bulgarian, Romanian, and Soviet (later, Russian) teams. At the world and Olympic level, Soviet teams have won more titles, both men's and women's, than those of any other nation. Their success was attributed to widespread grassroots interest and well-organized play and instruction at all levels of skill. A highly publicized Japanese women's team, Olympic champions in 1964, reflected the interest of private industry in sport. Young women working for the sponsoring company devoted their free time to conditioning, team practice, and competition under expert and demanding coaching. Encouraged by the Japanese Volleyball Association, this women's team made its mark in international competition, winning the World Championship in 1962, 1966, and 1967, in addition to the 1964 Olympics. At the end of the 20th century, however, the Cuban women's team dominated both the World Championships and the Olympics.

The Pan American Games (involving South, Central, and North America) added volleyball in 1955, and Brazil, Mexico,

Canada, Cuba, and the United States are frequent contenders for top honours. In Asia, China, Japan, and Korea dominate competition. Volleyball, especially beach volleyball, is played in Australia, New Zealand, and throughout the South Pacific.

A four-year cycle of international volleyball events, recommended by the FIVB, began in 1969 with World Cup championships, to be held in the year following the Olympic Games; the second year is the World Championships; in the third the regional events are held (e.g., European championships, Asian Games, African Games, Pan American Games); and in the fourth year the Olympic Games.

Beach volleyball—usually played, as its name implies, on a sand court with two players per team—was introduced in California in 1930. The first official beach volleyball tournament was held in 1948 at Will Rogers State Beach, in Santa Monica, California, and the first FIVB-sanctioned world championship was held in 1986 at Rio de Janeiro. Beach volleyball was added to the roster of the 1996 Olympic Games in Atlanta, Georgia.

The Game

Volleyball requires a minimum of equipment and space and can be played indoors or outdoors. The game is played on a smooth-surfaced court 9 metres (30 feet) wide by 18 metres (60 feet) long, divided by a centre line into two equal areas, one of which is selected by or assigned to each of the two competing teams.

Players may not step completely beyond the centre line while the ball is in play. A line 3 metres (10 feet) from and parallel to the centre line of each half of the court indicates the point in front of which a back court player may not drive the ball over the net from a position above the top of the net. (This offensive action, called a spike, or kill, is usually performed most effectively and with greatest power near the net by the forward line of players.) A tightly stretched net is placed across the court exactly above the middle of the centre line; official net heights (measured from the top edge of the net to the playing surface—in the middle of the court) are 2.4 metres (8 feet) for men and 2.2 metres (7.4 feet) for women.

Further adjustments in net height can be made for young people and others who need a lower net. A vertical tape marker is attached to the net directly above each side boundary line of the court, and, to help game officials judge whether served or volleyed balls are in or out of bounds, a flexible antenna extends 1 metre (3 feet) above the net along the outer edge of each vertical tape marker.

The ball used is around 260 to 280 grams (9 to 10 ounces) and is inflated to about 65 cm (25.6 inches) in circumference. A ball must pass over the net entirely between the antennae. A service area, traditionally 3 metres (10 feet) long, is marked outside and behind the right one-third of each court end line. At the 1996 Olympic Games the service area was extended to 9 metres (30 feet). The service must be made from within or behind this area. A space at least 2 metres (6 feet) wide around the entire court is needed to permit freedom of action, eliminate hazards from obstructions, and allow space for net support posts and the officials' stands. A clear area above the court at least 8 metres (26 feet) high is required to permit the ball to be served or received and played without interference.

The server stands at the back of the serving area. As the server moves toward the service line, the ball is tossed in front of and above the server. As the server leaps, the forearm rises to shoulder height, and the striking hand is drawn back. At the peak of the jump, the striking arm swings quickly forward with the open hand making contact with the ball out in front of the body.*Encyclopædia Britannica, Inc.*

volleyball passForearm passFrom the basic defensive position (knees bent, feet spread, one foot slightly in front of the other), the outstretched arms are brought together with thumbs together and rotated downward. The ball is met by the forearms with a shoveling motion of the arms. The pass should be made with a flowing, coordinated motion of the legs, body, and arms.*Encyclopædia Britannica, Inc.*

volleyball setFront setThe set is essentially a refined overhand pass. With elbows out, the hands should be raised to a position above the head. Palms should be out with fingers spread and thumbs down. The arms should extend to meet the ball with the pads of the fingers. The ball is directed upward and toward a spot where the hitter can make an aggressive play on it.*Encyclopædia Britannica, Inc.*

volleyball blockBlockPositioned about an arm's length from the net and ready to jump, the defender follows the flight of the ball with hands raised. The defender moves toward the net and into a blocking position in front of the presumed attacker. The defender then jumps, with both hands breaking the plane above the net.*Encyclopædia Britannica, Inc.*

volleyball digDigFrom the basic defensive position (knees bent, feet spread, one foot slightly in front of the other), the outstretched arms are brought together while the athlete lunges toward and under the ball in order to pop it back into the air with the hands or arms. If sprawling is necessary, the athlete follows through with a dive or a roll and quickly regains a standing position.*Encyclopædia Britannica, Inc.*

Informally, any number can play volleyball. In competition each team consists of six players, three of whom take the forward positions in a row close to and facing the net, the other three playing the back court. (An exception to this rotation is the *libero*, a position introduced at the 2000 Olympics) Play is started when the right back (the person on the right of the second row) of the serving team steps outside his end line into the serving area and bats the ball with a hand, fist, or arm over the net into the opponents' half of the court. The opponents receive the ball and return it across the net in a series of not more than three contacts with the ball. This must be done without any player catching or holding the ball while it is in play and without any player touching the net or entering the opponents' court area. The ball must not touch the floor, and a player may not touch the ball twice in succession. A player continues to serve until his team makes an error, commits a foul, or completes the game. When the service changes, the receiving team becomes the serving team and its players rotate clockwise one position, the right forward shifting to the right back position and then serving from the service area. Either team can score, with points being awarded for successfully hitting the ball onto the opposing side's half of the court, as well as when the opposing side commits errors or fouls, such as hitting the ball out of bounds, failing to return the ball, contacting the ball more than three times before returning it, etc. Only one point at a time is scored for a successful play. A game is won by the team that first scores 25 points, provided the winning team is ahead by 2 or more points, except in the fifth set, when a team needs to score only 15 points and win by 2 points.

The 2000 Olympics introduced significant rule changes to international competition. One change created the *libero*, a player on each team who serves as a defensive specialist. The *libero* wears a different colour from the rest of the team and is not allowed to serve or rotate to the front line. Another important rule change allowed the defensive side to score, whereas formerly only the serving team was awarded points.

HISTORY OF VOLLEYBALL

The sport originated in the United States, and is now just achieving the type of popularity in the U.S. that it has received on a global basis, where it ranks behind only soccer among participation sports.

Today there are more than 46 million Americans who play volleyball.

There are 800 million players worldwide who play Volleyball at least once a week.

1895, William G. Morgan, an instructor at the Young Men's Christian Association (YMCA) in Holyoke, Mass., decided to blend elements of basketball, baseball, tennis, and handball to create a game for his classes of businessmen which would demand less physical contact than basketball. He created the game of Volleyball (at that time called mintonette). Morgan borrowed the net from tennis, and raised it 6 feet 6 inches above the floor, just above the average man's head.

During a demonstration game, someone remarked to Morgan that the players seemed to be volleying the ball back and forth over the net, and perhaps "volleyball" would be a more descriptive name for the sport.

1896, July 7th - at Springfield College the first game of "volleyball" was played.

1900, a special ball was designed for the sport.

1900 - YMCA spread volleyball to Canada, the Orient, and the Southern Hemisphere.

1905 - YMCA spread volleyball to Cuba

1907 Volleyball was presented at the Playground of America convention as one of the most popular sports

1909 - YMCA spread volleyball to Puerto Rico

1912 - YMCA spread volleyball to Uruguay

1913 - Volleyball competition held in Far Eastern Games

1916, in the Philippines, an offensive style of passing the ball in a high trajectory to be struck by another player (the set and spike) were introduced. The Filipinos developed the "bomba" or kill, and called the hitter a "bomberino".

1916 - The NCAA was invited by the YMCA to aid in editing the rules and in promoting the sport. Volleyball was added to school and college physical education and intramural programs.

1917 - YMCA spread volleyball to Brazil

1917, the game was changed from 21 to 15 points.

1919 American Expeditionary Forces distributed 16,000 volleyballs to it's troops and allies. This provided a stimulus for the growth of volleyball in foreign lands.

1920, three hits per side and back row attack rules were instituted.

1922, the first YMCA national championships were held in Brooklyn, NY. 27 teams from 11 states were represented.

1928, it became clear that tournaments and rules were needed, the United States Volleyball Association (USVBA, now USA Volleyball) was formed. The first U.S. Open was staged, as the field was open to non-YMCA squads.

1930's Recreational sports programs became an important part of American life

1930, the first two-man beach game was played.

1934, the approval and recognition of national volleyball referees.

1937, at the AAU convention in Boston, action was taken to recognize the U.S. Volleyball Association as the official national governing body in the U.S.

Late 1940s Forearm pass introduced to the game (as a desperation play). Most balls were played with overhand pass.

1946 A study of recreation in the United States showed that volleyball ranked fifth among team sports being promoted and organized

1947, the Federation Internationale De Volley-Ball (FIVB) was founded in Paris.

1948, the first two-man beach tournament was held.

1949, the first World Championships were held in Prague, Czechoslovakia.

1949 USVBA added a collegiate division, for competitive college teams. For the first ten years collegiate competition was sparse. Teams formed only through the efforts of interested students and instructors. Many teams dissolved when the interested individuals left the college. Competitive teams were scattered, with no collegiate governing bodies providing leadership in the sport.

1951 - Volleyball was played by over 50 million people each year in over 60 countries

1955 - Pan American Games included volleyball

1957 - The International Olympic Committee (IOC) designated volleyball as an Olympic team sport, to be included in the 1964 Olympic Games.

1959 - International University Sports Federation (FISU) held the first University Games in Turin, Italy. Volleyball was one of the eight competitions held.

1960 Seven midwestern institutions formed the Midwest Intercollegiate Volleyball Association (MIVA)

1964 Southern California Intercollegiate Volleyball Association (SCVIA) was formed in California

1960's new techniques added to the game included - the soft spike (dink), forearm pass (bump), blocking across the net, and defensive diving and rolling.

In 1964, Volleyball was introduced to the Olympic Games in Tokyo.

The Japanese volleyball used in the 1964 Olympics, consisted of a rubber carcass with leather panelling. A similarly constructed ball is used in most modern competition.

In 1965, the California Beach Volleyball Association (CBVA) was formed.

1968 National Association of Intercollegiate Athletics (NAIA) made volleyball their fifteenth competitive sport.

1969 The Executive Committee of the NCAA proposed addition of volleyball to its program.

1974, the World Championships in Mexico were telecast in Japan.

1975, the US National Women's team began a year-round training regime in Pasadena, Texas (moved to Colorado Springs in 1979, Coto de Caza and Fountain Valley, CA in 1980, and San Diego, CA in 1985).

1977, the US National Men's team began a year-round training regime in Dayton, Ohio (moved to San Diego, CA in 1981).

1983, the Association of Volleyball Professionals (AVP) was formed.

1984, the US won their first medals at the Olympics in Los Angeles. The Men won the Gold, and the Women the Silver.

1986, the Women's Professional Volleyball Association (WPVA) was formed.

1987, the FIVB added a Beach Volleyball World Championship Series.

1988, the US Men repeated the Gold in the Olympics in Korea.

1989, the FIVB Sports Aid Program was created.

1990, the World League was created.

1992, the Four Person Pro Beach League was started in the United States.

1994, Volleyball World Wide, the first internet site on the sport of volleyball, was created.

1995, the sport of Volleyball was 100 years old!

1996, 2-person beach volleyball was added to the Olympics

There is a good book, *"Volleyball Centennial : The First 100 Years"*, available on the history of the sport.

EXERCISES

Here you will get some clues of how to practice the different skills in volleyball. You will also learn some exercises during the course, and you can try to invent some yourself. Do not be afraid of asking for advice if you see someone who manages what you are striving with. However, do not comment on anyone or give them advice before they ask for your opinion! Volleyball is supposed to be fun, and if team mates get angry with each other, it is not funny. There can be many ways of varying an exercise, and it should be adjusted to the skill level of the players. Remember: an exercise should be challenging, but not impossible!

Serve

Serving exercises can be lonely in the beginning. To run more complicated exercises, everyone has to manage the serve pretty well. If you do, you can start practising aiming towards a person or an item on the ground. Get together in pairs, one on each side of the net and serve to eachother. In the beginning, don't care about the borderline, but as you get better you can try serving from behind it.

A serving competition can include many players, each getting the same number of chances to serve. The one who gets the most serves over the net, has wone. The winner may give the others one advice about how they can improve their serves.

Fingerstroke/set

Practise in pairs passing to eachother. When receiving, strike once or twice straight up in the air – controling stroke – before passing the ball. Notice the different adjustments you have to make with your body position depending on if you are sending the ball straight up or forward.

When you start getting the hang of it, you can pass to eachother and touch the ground with your hands or sit down when the other player has the ball before receiving again.

Forehand pass/dig

Practise in pairs or three by three passing to eachother. As in fingerstroke, you can try controlling strokes in between, or sitting down quickly as soon as you have struck the ball.

If you are three players with one ball, one of you can be "the pusher" and pass to the two other who are in the opposite position. The pusher should vary by sending both long and short passes. The task is to get the ball as straight into the pusher's hands as possible. Here communication between the two "workers" is important to avoid crashes or noone taking the ball. Switch places after a while.

If you are three players with one ball, and really want a challenge, one player is "the worker" and the two others are "pushers". The worker moves sideways, gets a pass from the one ousher, passes it straight in the arms of the pusher, and moves sideways to the other pusher.

In this exercise the pushers hold the ball when they receive it. The worker has to remember to keep a low point of gravity. Switch places after e.g. 15 passes to the worker, as this exercise can be pretty exhausting.

This exercise can be developed further, by including more pushers, f.ex. standing by the net. Remember to vary the long and short strokes. The workers can line up in the corner of the field. When they are done withe receiving the ball, they can jog around the other part of the field, or move sideways along the other side of the net.

Spiking

In the beginning this can be difficult. Start by practicing the approaching steps and takeoff. This you can do together lined up in front of the net, or in pairs standing one on each side of the net. Remember to get both your hands up in the air.

If you start getting the hand of the rythm of spiking, you can try with a ball. One player, who is good at fingerstrokes, is the layer, standing by the net, a little to the right of the middle. The ones to spike line up on the sideedge of the court with one ball each. The ball is passed to the layer, who lays up, and the attacking player spikes the ball. This will take time to learn, be patient. In matches it is better to hit the ball over the net using another kind of stroke, if you are having problems with the spiking.

Playing exercises

A kind of playing exercise can be dividing the court in two, playing three by three players against eachother. You can make new rules, e.g. it is not allowed to send the ball over to the front 3 meters of the other team's court, or it is not allowed to spike.

The most important is not to win, but to keep the ball in the air for a long time.

A funny and popular exercise is called "paradise". Here there are three teams, only two playing at a time. Each ball is a deciding ball. One of the halfs of the court is paradise, it is where the teams gets to go if they win their game. In paradise, the points are counted if you win. The other half of the court is the challengers side. The team not playing is always the next challenger, and has to be ready immediately after the ball has hit the ground or been played out. The teams must try to get to the paradise side, or they cant get any points. The first team to reach 5,10 or 15 points, whatever you decide, wins. This is a great speedy exercise, once you understand it. It can be difficult in the beginning!

3

The Basic Rules of V olleyball

We have provided information about the basic rules of volleyball when watching your children play.

The Serve

1. Server must serve from behind the restraining line (end line) until after contact.
2. Ball may be served underhand or overhand.
3. Ball must be clearly visible to opponents before serve.
4. Served ball may graze the net and drop to the other side.
5. First game serve is determined by a coin toss. Game 2 will be served by the receiving team in game 1. If match goes to a 3rd game, new coin toss will determine serving team.
6. If best of 5 game match: Game 2, 3, an 4 will trade off between teams. If teams go to game 5, serve will go to winner of a new coin toss.
7. Serve must be returned by a pass or set only. Serve can not be blocked or attacked.

Scoring

1. Rally scoring- which means there will be a point awarded on every won rally.
2. Offense will score on a defensive miss, out of bounds hit, or blocker touches the top of the net.

3. Defense will score on an offensive miss, out of bounds hit, serve into the net or hitter touches top of the net.

4. Game will be played to 25 pts. Game 3 is played to 15.

5. Must win by 2 points, unless a point cap has been placed.

Rotation

1. Team will rotate after each sideout. A sideout is when the team on serve receive wins the point to earn the right to serve.

2. Players shall rotate in a clockwise manner.

3. There shall be 6 players on each side.

Playing The Game (Volley)

1. Maximum of three hits per side.

2. Player may not hit the ball twice in succession (A block is not considered a hit).

3. Ball may be played off the net during a volley and on serve.

4. A ball touching any part of the boundary line is considered in.

5. A legal hit is contact with the ball by any part of the players body which does not allow the ball to visibly come to a rest.

6. A player must not block or attack a serve.

Basic Violations

1. Stepping on or over the line on a serve.

2. Failure to serve the ball over the net successfully.

3. Hitting the ball illegally (Carrying, Palming, Throwing, etc.).

4. Touches of the top of the net only with any part of the body while the ball is in play. Players may contact the net below the top of the net (the tape) at any time. If the ball is driven into the net with such force that it causes the net

to contact an opposing player, no foul will be called, and the ball shall continue to be in play.

5. Reaching over the net, except under these conditions:

   - 1 - When executing a follow-through.
   - 2 - When blocking a ball which is in the opponents court but is being returned (the blocker must not contact the ball until after the opponent who is attempting to return the ball makes contact). Except to block the third play.

     1. Reaches under the net (if it interferes with the ball or opposing player).
     2. Failure to serve in the correct order.
     3. Blocks or spikes from a position which is clearly not behind the 10-foot line while in a back row position.
     4. A players foot may not completely cross the midline at any time. However, if the rest of the body crosses it is legal unless interferes with a player on the other side of the net.

Substitutions

1. Coaches only have 12 substitutions per game in club.
2. Once a player subs in for a rotational position, they can only sub in for that rotational position.

RULES

The rules of volleyball are simple, but they're constantly changing, and they can differ depending on the level of competition. I started playing volleyball in middle school, in 2000, and since then, several changes have affected high school and collegiate rules.

Setting up the Court

A volleyball court is 30 feet wide and 60 feet long; each side of the net is 30 feet by 30 feet. A 2-inch line borders the court to serve as the out-of-bounds line. Any ball that touches the line during play is still considered "in" the court. In volleyball, there are six people on the court at one time for each team. Usually three people are in the front row, and three are in the back row. The front row is sectioned off by a line 10 feet from the net, called the "attack line" or the "10-foot line." Front-row players are not confined to this section of the court, but this is where most of their playing takes place.

Back to Basics

One thing that stays constant despite rule changes, though, is that during each possession on one side of the net, a team can only have three contacts with the ball. The ideal sequence of contacts is usually a pass, a set and a hit—even the terminology has changed over the years. These skills were traditionally called bump, set and spike.

No player can ever make contact with the ball twice in succession, and the ball cannot be caught or carried over the net. A block is not considered as part of a hit, which I'll explain in the ADVANCED section. Each play starts off with a serve. The server steps behind the line at the very back of the court, called the end line, and has freedom to serve from wherever he or she pleases as long as the foot does not touch or cross the line. If the server's foot crosses the end line, it is considered a foot fault, and results in a side-out—a change in possession—of the ball.

The server must make the ball go over the net on the serve. It doesn't matter if the ball touches the net on a serve anymore. Balls that hit the net on serves and still go over and stay in the court used to be illegal, but now they are allowed. These serves are called "let serves."

Rotation

Positions are numbered, one through six, starting with the server in the back right corner. Then going in a counter-clockwise direction, the rest of the positions are numbered. The actual direction of the rotation is clockwise, however. After the server finishes, the other team gets the ball, and you get the ball back, everyone just shifts to the right one spot.

Rotation, if not fully understood, can be a very confusing part of the game. In basic volleyball there are three players in the front row and three in the back, and each player just rotates to the next position as the plays go along. Any time a player is in the back row, he or she cannot "attack" the ball in front of the 10-foot line on the court.

Attacks are also known as "hits" or "spikes"—usually the third hit of a possession. This rule is in effect to make sure that the strong hitters aren't always able to dominate the game. When the strong hitters are in the back row, they can still attack the ball on the third hit, but they cannot jump in front of the 10-foot line.

Switching

Contrary to the way it may seem, there are actually positions in volleyball, and despite the mandatory rotation, it's possible to play the same position every play. The only catch is that if you're not already in the position where you want to be, you have to wait to move to that spot until after the ball has gone over the net on a serve.

Many teams use a hand-linking system to make the switch easier, but no player can cross another's plane of rotation until the ball goes over the net.

Scoring

As for scoring, this has also changed. When I first started playing, points could only be scored by the serving team, and games went to 15 points. Matches consisted of the best two out of three games.

Now volleyball has changed to rally scoring. Essentially, teams score points whenever the other team messes up, and a point is awarded on every serve. Depending on the level of competition, most matches are now played as the best three out of five games to 25 points. Teams must win by at least two points for games to end. Points keep going until one team wins with a margin of victory of two points even if the score is greater than 25.

BASIC VOLLEYBALL RULES

Basic Rules and Procedures

Not knowing the basic volleyball rules can be a frustrating experience whether you're a player, coach, or just a fan.

You may have stumbled upon volleyball on television. You're watching the game, the referees make a call, and you don't understand why.

Maybe you have a sudden interest in volleyball now that your daughter has made the high school volleyball team. You want to understand the rules the best you can so you can cheer her team on.

Maybe you're a player that often gets frustrated when a referee makes a call that you don't understand.

Maybe you're coaching and looking for every advantage you can get to help your team win.

Maybe you're a recreational volleyball player that is looking for that edge you need.

Whether you're a coach, athlete, parent, fan, or just a recreational player, it's a good idea to be familiar with the basic volleyball rules.

Basic Volleyball Rules for Playing the Game

- 6 players on a team, 3 on the front row and 3 on the back row
- Maximum of three hits per side
- Player may not hit the ball twice in succession (A block is not considered a hit)
- Ball may be played off the net during a volley and on a serve

- A ball hitting a boundary line is "in"
- A ball is "out" if it hits...
- an antennae,
- the floor completely outside the court,
- any of the net or cables outside the antennae,
- the referee stand or pole,
- the ceiling above a nonplayable area
- It is legal to contact the ball with any part of a players body
- It is illegal to catch, hold, or throw the ball
- If two or more players contact the ball at the same time, it is considered one play and either player involved may make the next contact (provided the next contact isn't the teams 4th hit)
- A player can not block or attack a serve from on or inside the 10 foot line
- After the serve, front line players may switch positions at the net
- At higher competition, the officiating crew may be made up of two refs, line judges, scorer, and an assistant scorer

Basic Volleyball Rules Violations

The result of a violation is a point for the opponent.

- When serving, stepping on or across the service line as you make contact with the serve
- Failure to serve the ball over the net successfully
- Contacting the ball illegally (lifting, carrying, throwing, etc.)
- Touching the net with any part of the body while the ball is in play. Exception: If the ball is driven into the net with such force that it causes the net to contact an opposing player, no foul will be called, and the ball shall continue to be in play.

- When blocking a ball coming from the opponents court, contacting the ball when reaching over the net is a violation if both:

  1) your opponent hasn't used 3 contacts AND

  2) they have a player there to make a play on the ball

- When attacking a ball coming from the opponents court, contacting the ball whenreaching over the net is a violation if the ball hasn't yet broken the vertical plane of the net.

- Crossing the court centerline with any part of your body. Exception: if it's the hand or foot, the entire hand or entire foot must cross for it to be a violation.

- Serving out of order.

- Back row player blocking (deflecting a ball coming from their opponent), when at the moment of contact the back row player is near the net and has part of his/her body above the top of the net (an illegal block).

- Back row player attacking a ball inside the front zone (the area inside the 10 foot line), when at the moment of contact the ball is completely above the net (an illegal attack).

BASIC VOLLEYBALL GAME RULES

Volleyball is a complex game of simple skills. The ball is spiked from up to 60 cm above the height of a basketball hoop (about 3.65 metres) and takes fractions of a second to travel from the spiker to the receiver. That means the receiver must assess incoming angle, decide where to pass the ball and then control their pass in the blink of an eye. A purely rebound sport (you can't hold the ball), volleyball is a game of constant motion.

A team can touch the ball three times on its side of the net. The usual pattern is a dig (an underarm pass made with the forearms), a set (an overhead pass made with the hands) and a spike (the overhead attacking shot). The ball is served into play. Teams can also try to block the opponent's spike as it crosses the net. A block into your own court counts as one of your three touches in beach volleyball, but not in volleyball.

Power and height have become vital components of international teams, but the ability of teams and coaches to devise new strategies, tactics and skills has been crucial for continued success.

- There are six players on court in a volleyball team, who each must rotate one position clockwise every time their team wins back service from the opposition. Only the three players at the net positions can jump and spike or block near the net. The backcourt players can only hit the ball over the net if they jump from behind the attack line, also known as the three-metre line, which separates the front and back part of the court.

- Volleyball has developed into a very specialised sport. Most teams will include in their starting line-up a setter, two centre blockers, two receiver-hitters and a universal spiker. Only certain players will be involved with service reception. Players will also have specialist positions for attack and defence. Substitutions are allowed during the game.

- Since 1998, volleyball bas been using a new scoring system. Teams scored a point on every rally (Rally Point System), regardless of which team served. Formerly, a team could only win a point if it served the ball. Winning the serve back from the opposition was known as a side-out.

- Matches are played best of five sets. The first four sets are played to 25 points, with the final set being played to 15 points. A team must win a set by two points. There is no ceiling, so a set continues until one of the teams gains a two-point advantage. Previously, all sets were to 15 points, with the first four sets having a ceiling of 17 and the final set requiring at least a two-point winning advantage.

- In 1998, the FIVB introduced a new specialist role: the libero. This player wears a different coloured uniform from the rest of the team and can be substituted in backcourt for any player on the team. The libero cannot serve, spike the ball over the net or rotate into the front-line positions, but plays a vital role for the team in serve reception and backcourt defence. There must be at least one point played between a libero substituting off for a player and going back on the court for another player – hence he/she cannot be on the court for the whole game. The libero has added an extra dimension to backcourt defence, improving the reception of teams, lengthening the rallies and giving a vital role to shorter players.

VOLLEYBALL 101: RULES

A volleyball match begins when the ball is served into play. A team may touch the ball three times (not counting blocks) on its side of the net, the usual pattern being a dig (an underarm pass made with the forearms), a set (an overhead pass made with the hands) and a spike (the overhead attacking shot). Teams also try to block the opponent's spike as it crosses the net.

ROTATION

Starting line-up

A team's coach presents the starting line-up to the referees before the start of every set. The starting line-up indicates the rotational order of the players on the court. This order must be maintained throughout the set. At any given time there must be six players in play on each team. The players who are not in the starting line-up are the substitutes for that set (except for the libero, who can be substituted at any time).

Positions

The three players along the net are front row players and occupy positions 4 (front left), 3 (front center), and 2 (front right). The other three are back row players occupying positions 5 (back left), 6 (back center), and 1 (back right). At the moment the ball is hit by the server, each team (except the server) must be positioned within its own court in the rotational order. After the service is hit, the players may move around and occupy any position on their court or in the free zone. The team commits a rotational fault (loss of the point) if any player is not in his or her correct position when the serve is executed.

Order

Rotational order is determined by the team's starting line-up, and controlled with the service order, throughout the set. When the receiving team has gained the right to serve, its players rotate one position clockwise: the player in position 2 rotates to position 1 to serve, the player in position 1 rotates to position 6, etc.

In or out?

The ball is "in" when it touches the floor of the playing court — boundary lines are considered part of the playing court. The ball is "out" when:

The part of the ball touching the floor is completely outside the boundary lines.

It touches an object outside the court, the ceiling, or a person out of play.

It touches the antennae, ropes, posts or the net itself outside the side bands.

It crosses the vertical plane of the net partially or totally outside the crossing space.

It crosses the lower space under the net.

Serving

Coin toss

The first referee carries out a coin toss to determine the first service and the sides of the court in the first set (and in a deciding set, if one is to be played). The winner of the toss can choose either the right to serve or receive the service, or which side of the court to play on. The loser takes the remaining choice. For sets two through four, the team that did not serve first in the previous set serves first, and it alternates again for the next set.

Order

After the initial service in the set, players serve by rotating in the order of the starting line-up. When the serving team wins the rally, the player (or his/her substitute) who served before serves again. When the receiving team wins the rally, it gains the right to serve and rotates before actually serving. The player who moves from the front right position to the back-right position serves.

Execution

The ball must be hit with one hand or any part of the arm after being tossed or released from the hand or hands. Only one toss or release of the ball is allowed. At the moment of the service hit (or take-off for a jump service), the server must not touch the court (the end line included) or the ground outside the service zone. After the hit, he may step or land outside the service zone or inside the court. The server must hit the ball within 8 seconds after the first referee whistles for service. Screening is not allowed and is grounds for a service fault. A player or group of players of the serving team make a screen by waving arms, jumping or moving sideways during a serve, or by standing grouped to hide the flight path of the ball.

Service faults

- The serve touches a player of the serving team.
- The serve fails to cross the vertical plane of the net between the antennae.
- The serve lands "out."

Hits

A team is allowed to make a maximum of three hits to return the ball. Hits include intentional and unintentional contacts with the ball — a deflection off a block is not counted as a team hit.

The ball must be hit, not caught or thrown. The ball may touch any part of the body, or various parts of the body provided that the contacts take place simultaneously. There is an exception in blocking provided that the contacts occur during one action — that is, if a blocker deflects an attack into the air, he or she may then hit the ball again.

Two or three players may touch the ball simultaneously. With the exception of blocking, when two (or three) players touch the ball simultaneously, it is counted as two (or three) hits. When two opponents touch the ball simultaneously over the net and the ball remains in play, the team receiving the ball is entitled to another three hits. If the ball goes out, it is the fault of the team which hit it. If simultaneous contacts by two opponents leads to a "lift" fault, it is a "double fault" and the rally is replayed.

Hitting faults

- Four hits: More than three hits are used by one team.
- Double contact: A player hits the ball twice in succession or the ball contacts various parts of his/her body in succession.
- Lift: A player does not hit the ball, and the ball is caught and/or thrown.
- Assisted hit: A player takes support from a teammate or any structure/object in order to reach the ball within the playing area.

Attacks

Excluding serves and blocks, any action that involves directing the ball over the net toward the opponent's court is an attack hit.

Restrictions

A front-row player may complete an attack hit at any height, provided the contact with the ball has been made within the player's own playing space. A back-row player may complete an attack hit from anywhere behind the front zone, provided his or her feet are behind the attack line, or were behind the attack line upon jumping. After the attack hit, the player may land within the front zone. A back-row player may execute an attack hit from the front zone, if at the moment of contact the ball is not entirely higher than the top of the net.

Attacking faults

- A player hits the ball within the playing space of the opposing team.
- A player hits the ball "out."
- A back-row player completes an attack hit from the front zone and the ball is entirely higher than the top of the net at the moment of the hit.
- A libero completes an attack hit if at the moment of the hit the ball is entirely higher than the top of the net.
- A player completes an attack hit on the opponent's service when the ball is in the front zone and entirely higher than the top of the net (in other words, no blocking a serve).

Blocking

Blocking occurs when a player or players at the net attempt to prevent an opponent's attack hit from making it past a front line of defense and into a team's playing area. Only front-row players are permitted to complete a block. A collective block is executed by two or three players close to each other and is completed when one of them touches the ball. Consecutive contacts may occur by one or more blockers provided that the contacts are made during one action. In blocking, the player may place his or her hands and arms beyond the net provided that this does not interfere with the opponent's play; therefore, it is not permitted to touch the ball beyond the net until an opponent has executed an attack hit.

Block and team hits

A block contact is not counted as a team hit. After a block contact, a team is entitled to three hits to return the ball. The first hit after the block may be executed by any player, including the one who executed the block.

Blocking faults

- The blocker touches the ball in the opponent's space before or simultaneously with the opponent's attack hit.
- A back row player or a libero completes a block or participates in a completed block.
- Blocking the opponent's serve.
- A blocked ball lands "out."

Coaching

Throughout a match, the coach conducts a team's play from outside the playing court. During a match, the coach requests timeouts and substitutions. He or she may give instructions to the players on the court while standing or walking within the free zone in front of his or her team's bench, as long as he or she doesn't disturb or delay the match. The assistant coach sits on the team bench but cannot intervene in the match. Should the coach leave the team, the assistant coach may assume the coach's functions at the request of the team captain.

Substitution

In substitution, a player enters the game to occupy the position of another player (except the libero) who leaves the court. Substitution requires the referee's authorization, and only the coach or the game captain can request a substitution. Each team is entitled to six substitutions per set. One or more players may be substituted at the same time.

Starters

A player from the starting line-up may be substituted for once per set. He or she may re-enter — only to his or her previous position — but must then remain at least until the end of the set. A substitute may enter the game once per set, and can only be substituted by the same starter he or she replaced.

Exceptional substitution

An injured player (except the libero) who cannot continue should be substituted. If this is not possible — for instance, if the player already had been substituted for earlier in the same set — the team is entitled to make an exceptional substitution, meaning that any player who is not on the court at the time of the injury can substitute into the game for the injured player. The injured player is not allowed to re-enter the match after the exceptional substitute has entered the game.

Disqualified players

An expelled or disqualified player must be substituted.

Timeouts

Each team is entitled to request a maximum of two timeouts per set. All requested timeouts last 30 seconds. A timeout request is made with a hand signal (forming a "T" using both hands) when the ball is out of play and before the whistle for service. A technical time-out of 60 seconds is applied automatically when the leading team reaches the eighth and 16th points in sets one through four. There are no technical time-outs in the deciding (fifth) set, only each team's two 30-second time-outs.

Misconduct

Minor misconduct is not subject to sanctions. Misconduct that leads to sanctions is classified in three categories according to the seriousness of the offense:

Rude conduct: action contrary to good manners or moral principles, or expressing contempt.

Offensive conduct: defamatory or insulting words or gestures.

Aggression: physical attack or intended aggression.

Sanction scale

Depending on the seriousness of the offense, the first referee will apply one of the following sanctions:

Penalty (yellow card)

The first "rude conduct" in the match by any team member is penalized with the loss of rally.

Expulsion (red card)

A player or coach sanctioned by expulsion must remain seated in the penalty area for the remainder of the set at hand. The following are grounds for expulsion:

- The first "offensive conduct" by a team member.
- The second "rude conduct" in the same match, by the same team member.

Disqualification (yellow and red card jointly)

Player disqualification occurs for:

- The first "aggression".
- The second "offensive conduct" in the same match by the same team member.
- The third "rude conduct" in the same match by the same team member.

4

Volleyball Variations

Variations of the game volleyball have been in circulation since around 1895. The game has evolved since then and it was in 1964 where the sport entered its first Olympic games. The sport now has a global following with nations from around the world professionally competing. The pinnacle of the sport comes in the Olympic Games were the best players are often on show.

Object of the Game

The object of volleyball is to hit the volleyball over the net (by only using your hands) running through the centre of the court whilst trying to get it to bounce in your opponents half. The opposing team have to try and prevent the ball from bouncing before returning the ball. Games are played out in best of 3 or 5 sets and the team with most sets at the end of the game wins.

Players & Equipment

Each team has 6 players on a court at any one time. Substitutes can be used throughout the game. There are no professional mixed sex teams. Each player takes up a position in either the attacking zone (next to the net) or the defensive zone (at the back of the court). Three players are in each zone and rotate in a clockwise position after every point.

The court is of a rectangular shape and measures 18m x 9m. Running across the court is a 2.43m high net with the ball measuring 8 inches in diameter and weighing between 9 and 10 ounces. Around the outlines of the court is an out of bounds area and if the ball were to bounce in these sections then a point would be awarded to the opposing team.

Each team gets up to two timeouts per set of 30 seconds each. After each set the amount of timeouts resets back to two regardless of how many have been used previously.

Scoring

To score a point the ball must hit the ground within the outlined section in your opponents half. You can also score a point by your opponent failing to hit the outlined section within your half or your opponent hitting the ball into the net. A point can be scored off either teams serve.

A player serving must do so from behind the base line and can use either an over or underarm action and hit with only the hand. Once the serve has been made the sever can join their team in-play and battle out the point.

Each team is allowed to hit the ball three times before the ball must be returned. A player is not allowed to hit the ball twice in succession.

If the ball hits the boundary line then the ball is deemed to be in-play. The defensive team can jump and try to block the ball returning to their side of the court. If a block attempt is made and the ball bounces in their opponents half then a point is awarded. If after the block the ball bounces out then a point is awarded to the opposing team.

Each game is played to 25 points and must be two points clear. If the scores reach 24-24 then the game is played until one team leads by two.

Winning the Game

To win the game you must score more points than your opponents. The best of 3 or 5 sets are generally played and the winners will be the first team to reach the required number of sets.

Rules of Volleyball

- Each team consist of 6 players and 6 substitutes. Players can be substituted at any time but if they are to return can only be swapped for the player that replaced them.

- Each team can hit the ball up to three times before the ball must be returned. The defensive team can then try and block or return the ball again hitting it a maximum of three times.

- Games are played up to 25 points and must be won by 2 clear points.

- Violations will be called for the following:
  - Stepping over the base line when serving the ball.
  - Ball hits the net and fails to get over the net (If the ball hits the net and still goes over the net then this is perfectly legal).
  - Players are not allowed to carry, palm or run with the ball.
  - Players must not touch the net with any part of the body. If the net is said to have hit them rather than vice-versa, then this is ok.
  - The ball cannot travel under the net.
  - Players cannot reach over the net and hit the ball.

Beach volleyball

A variation of the game rivaling the original sport of volleyball in popularity, beach volleyball evolved from the recreational games of volleyball played on many beaches around the world. It became an official Olympic sport in 1996. This version, rather than being played on indoor hard courts, is played on sand courts which may either be formed naturally or built specifically for the purpose.

Instead of a team of six, each team consists of only two players, but otherwise the rules are almost identical with some exceptions including:

- The size of the court (16m x 8m)
- The block counts as the first contact

Rows of beach volleyball nets in Huntington Beach, California.

- The banning of the open-hand *dink* or *dump* plays where a player uses his or her finger tips to redirect the ball into the opponent's court instead of a hard spike. A dink may be performed with a closed hand or knuckle
- Stricter rules around double-contacts during hand setting
- The time limit for serve is 5 seconds
- Games are usually played to 21 points, rather than 25 as common in indoor volleyball. The first team to win two sets wins the match. If a third deciding set is required, it is played to 15.

Indoor sand volleyball

This is a newer variation of beach volleyball. As beach volleyball took volleyball outdoors, indoor sand volleyball takes beach volleyball indoors. In the United States, a growing number of colleges are now considering switching from hard court indoor volleyball to sand court indoor volleyball. The biggest reason for the possible change is the reduced rate of injury of players. Secondary reasons are: 1) bad weather doesn't cancel play, something that commonly happens with beach volleyball; 2) it is thought to make the game more appealing to spectators since sand courts do not require players to wear knee pads or shoes.

Indoor sand volleyball teams vary from two to six members, college teams having six. Normally, rather than using a purpose-built hall, an indoor basketball court is converted. A protective tarpaulin covers the floor of the basketball court and "soft" sand is laid a foot deep over it.

The boundaries are commonly marked off with lines in the sand. However, a recent innovation uses colored lasers that illuminate the lines in the sand.

In some venues, there exist sand courts that are used as usual during the spring, summer, and fall months, but during the winter months, a large tent (usually dome-shaped) is erected over the courts.

Snow volleyball

A variant of beach volleyball that is played on snow. The tactics and rules are similar to beach volleyball, but due to the different playing surface, players wear cleats during matches.

Snow volleyball first gained popularity in Wagrain, Austria, in 2008. It was recognized as an official sport by the Austrian Volleyball Association in 2011. The European Volleyball Confederation (CEV) officially added the sport and organized the first snow volleyball European tour in 2016. The inaugural Snow Volleyball European Championships is planned for 2018. The Fédération Internationale de Volleyball (FIVB) has announced its plans to make snow volleyball part of the future Winter Olympic Games programme. At the 2018 Winter Olympics, the FIVB and the CEV recruited beach volleyball Olympians to compete in a demonstration at the Austria House.

SHOOTING VOLLEYBALL

In shooting volleyball the team consists of normally seven players. Three players play at the back side, three players play center of the court, and one player stands in front of the net. Any ball that goes to into the net is to be out by the player who is standing in front of it, also known as the net man. Some players also smash the ball with high vertical leaps like Olympic volleyball but there is no setter in team. In this game, the players hit the ball with both hands by punching it with both hands. They try to hit as fast as they can in order to force a mistake from opponent players and try to get rebound as a set ball for any player to smash it with jump, using one hand and if the player standing under the net misses the ball than defender tries to take the ball using the under hand and give maximum height to it. When one player smashes the ball with great skill the spectators give prize money to that player and the game has to stop at that time.

Shooting volleyball court is 35 ft and 70 ft in length. Net height was 8 ft before some years but nowadays the net height is 7.2 ft to 7.5 ft (2.20m). The ball size is same to handball. Shooting volleyball is popular in Pakistan (Punjab)(Sindh)(Bloachistan) (KPK), USA and India, especially North Indian States. Most of the above-mentioned rules are not valid at present in shooting volleyball(Pakistan). For example:The height of net has reduced to 6.0 feet. Nowadays eight players can play in a team four players play at back side and four at the center of court and one player stands in front of net. If any ball goes into net (called as 3rd ball or 'common ball'), the net man pushes it back to his team and the 'Defencer' (man which is standing in the right center) pushes it towards the back side players (3rd players) of the opponent team. And the players of 3rd hit it forcefully.

In Northern India (Especially NCR Delhi Haryana Uttar-pradesh)

Length of the court is 32 (official)foot. and height of net varies area to area (7 to 8 ft). Nowadays, Northern players are playing

Dropping game, In which on Third ball player is not allowed to jump. he/she needs to remains on surface while playing third ball.

Third Ball Means, When Center Player hits ball into net and net men lift ball up, then next player who is sending that ball into opposite court, He/she need to make contact with ground while clearing that ball third ball.

Most of places Under handball touches net, then It is foul.

Net Man not allowed to lift under Handball which touches nets.

Footbag net

Footbag net is similar to sepak takraw and footvolley. It's played with feet instead of hands. Footbag net combines elements of tennis, badminton, and volleyball. Specifically, the court dimensions and layout are similar to those of badminton; the scoring is similar to the old scoring system in volleyball (you must be serving to score); and serves must be diagonal, as in tennis. It is played one on one or in teams of two. Footbag net games can be played to eleven or fifteen points, although the winners must win by at least two points.

Newcomb ball

A simplified form used to teach the fundamentals of volleyball, Newcomb (occasionally referred to as "Nuke 'em") is generally taught to school-aged children but is also popular among adults of limited athletic ability. Its main differences from regular volleyball are that the ball can be caught before passing on to a team-mate or over the net, and each pass or serve is a throw rather than a hit. While most other volleyball rules apply, variations on the numbers of players per team and the numbers of 'catches' per side are common, and players holding the ball are sometimes allowed a limited number of steps.

Newcomb (or Newcomb Ball) was invented in 1895 by Clara Gregory Baer, a physical education instructor at Newcomb College in Louisiana.

Volleyball was independently invented in the same year. Newcomb was a popular competitive sport in the early 1900s, but it is now seen as a variation of volleyball and is played mostly by school children.

Newcomb can be also played in a way similar to dodgeball. The main and only difference in the less played version is that instead of scoring points, a teammate is eliminated if he or she makes a mistake. The game continues until all of the players on one team are eliminated.

Sepak Takraw

Sepak Takraw is a variant of volleyball popular in Asia, similar to footvolley. The rules are very similar to those in volleyball, with the following four important exceptions: The use of hands is not permitted, each player may only touch the ball once before it is kicked back over the net, there is no rotation in the defence position and players use their feet to get the ball over the net. The game is played on a badminton doubles court. Another similar game played with the feet and originating in Thailand is Buka ball.

Footvolley

Footvolley is an entirely new sport which combines beach volleyball and soccer skills. The difference is that the players may not contact the ball with their hands or arms; instead they can use all other body parts including their feet, head and chest, etc. Sport originated in Brazil; but is quickly becoming popular in the US, Europe, and Asia.

SITTING VOLLEYBALL

Sitting volleyball for locomotor-disabled individuals was first introduced in 1956 by the Dutch Sports Committee. International competition began in 1967, but it would be 1978 before the International Sports Organisation for the Disabled (ISOD) sanctioned the sport and sponsored an official international tournament in 1979 at Haarlem, Netherlands.

The game is played on a smaller 10 x 6 meter court and with a 0.8 meter-wide net set to a height of 1.15 meters for men and 1.05 meters for women. When hitting or attacking the ball, the player must have one "buttock" or an extension of the torso still in contact with the floor. Traditionally the sport has been played not only by amputees and people with polio, but people who have orthopedic problems in their knees or ankles. Often players with no sitting volleyball classification are on the club teams. Because of the game's quick pace, the use of your hands to move and play the ball, good balance and a sturdy bottom are a necessity. Consequently, it is not the ideal sport for most paraplegics.

Men's sitting volleyball was introduced to the Paralympic Games in 1980 and has grown to be one of the more popular Paralympic sports due to the fast and exciting action. Women's sitting volleyball was added to the program for the 2004 Summer Paralympics in Athens, Greece. The international governing body for the sport is The World Organisation Volleyball for Disabled (WOVD). The WOVD was founded in 1980 in the Netherlands, by the Dutchman Pieter Joon.

Traditional Volleyball

Traditional volleyball has its roots in East Africa. The game is usually played within the Ithna Ashari, Ismaili, Bohra, Kokni, Punjabi, Rajput Dhobi, Lohana, Waniya, Kutchi communities worldwide. Traditional volleyball varies from indoor gymnasium play, outdoor play on sand, grass, or clay - as well as street volleyball for recreation.

There is a three-touch system like International volleyball, however, traditional volleyball does not require the bump-set-spike scenario. Instead, traditional volleyball is based on a consistent volley of the ball -only the serving side can score- and players play a style which is considered "closed hand/fist" play. The game can be played with up to nine participants per side (similar to Asian nine-man volleyball, but with variations to the game), or as little as five. There is no rotation in traditional volleyball, however, in certain East Indian and Southeast Asian communities, they do allow rotating as the rules tend to vary from team to team. The court can vary from 30' to 30' to as large as '35 by '35.

In North America, some of the best traditional volleyball teams are centered in Eastern Canada. This includes Toronto North, Toronto Jaffery's, RK's Golden Eagles, TVC, 786'ers, United Stars, and many more. Western Canada is also home to several teams, including Vancouver, Port Moody, Edmonton, and Calgary. The U.S. also boasts a number of teams that practice on a weekly basis, including Houston, Dallas, New York Union, New York Hydery, Allentown Challengers, Allentown Union, Orlando Union, Albuquerque, and other cities. The weight of the ball varies as well - in North America they play with a lighter ball, around 10.5-11 lbs. of pressure. However, in East Africa, India, and Pakistan, the game is played with a heavier ball, anywhere from 12 to 14 lbs. of pressure.

Some of the key positions on the team are Net Centre (or netty). He is responsible for lifting and/or digging the ball out of the net on a second touch. In the old days, the netty was encouraged to lift the ball up and over the net to the opposing team. As the years went by and the variant styles of the game were changing, the netty was encouraged to lift the ball back to his team so that they could strike the ball (third touch) to the opposing side and keep the volley going. There was usually one netty per team back in the old days. Today, teams are allowed to play with up to two nettys simultaneously, or even a third netty on the far right or left corners of the net-thus preventing an advantage of the opposing team to drop or 'dink' the ball. The short centre spot is a position that was previously called the 'sweeper'. This position was put into fruition in Canada some years ago, and the object of the short centre is to strike the ball into the net as much as he can, so that the netty can give a nice, high, clean lift to his team to strike back to the opposing side.

The third and probably most important position is the Long Centre (formerly third line). He controls the pace, tempo, and speed of the game - and is instrumental in taking points by a method called flights or shooting. Everyone else on the team, from the front line wings to the back line wings, as well as the serviceman also play crucial roles on the team. The serviceman is not allowed to serve overhand though, and spiking is not allowed on a third touch. Traditional Volleyball teams play in local, state, provincial, regional, national, and even international tournaments every year. From Dar es Salaam and Nairobi to Karachi and especially the U.K., the game is growing at rapid rates. In fact, more youth are now playing traditional volleyball than ever before. The hope is that someday this version of volleyball can be played at the Asian Games or even the Olympics.

Unlike the FIVB, there is no governing body for traditional volleyball. There was an attempt in the mid to late 1990s to form a North American league called TVANA - Traditional Volleyball Association of North America. This league had three successful tournaments in Houston before sadly folding. However, the league was instrumental in uniting U.S. and Canadian teams for the first time in years. The tournaments were also highly energetic, and helped usher lasting bonds of friendship, sportsmanship, and competitive play.

NINE-MAN VOLLEYBALL

A triple block in a game of nine-man volleyball

Nine-man volleyball is a variation of volleyball utilizing nine players and a slightly larger court (10 by 20 meters) originated in Asia in the 1920s when American missionaries introduced the game in China. The birthplace of 9man can be speculated to be the city of Tai-Shan, China where 9man tournaments are played regularly, sometimes even for prize money. 9man is also played for recreation in South Korea.

The variant became popular within the Chinese-American communities community in New York City and spread to Chinatowns other large US and Canadian cities. The North American version of 9man volleyball continues to grow with a rotating popular tournament called the North American Chinese Invitational Volleyball Tournament. It was played in the Asian Games in 1958 and in 1962.

Aside from the larger court and additional players, rule differences for 9man volleyball in Asia and of those used in the NACIVT differ.

The major rule differences from indoor volleyball and NACIVT 9man rules include (Those rules in italics only apply within NACIVT rules):

- A lower net (235 cm rather than 243).
- *Players don't rotate – front players stay in front (and thus never serve), and back players in back.*
- If the ball touches the net between two contacts by the same team, those two contacts only count as one of the three allowed before the ball must be sent over the net. The same player may legally make both contacts.
- *It is permitted to briefly carry the ball during a spiking motion.*
- *Players may not penetrate the plane of the net while blocking.*
- If a player touches the ball while blocking, it counts as one of the three allowed contacts.
- *Jump serving is illegal.*
- It is illegal to touch the ball with any body part besides the hands and arms.
- A served ball which hits the top of the net and falls inside the boundaries of the opponents' court entitles the server to a second chance (like tennis).
- There is no "ten foot line": any player may attack the ball from anywhere on the court.

9man rules used in Asia are slightly different:

- Players do not rotate, however every player on the court must serve at some point.
- Carrying or lifts are not legal.
- Players may penetrate the plane of the net when blocking.
- Jump-serving is legal.

In South Korea, nine-man volleyball is popular as a recreation. But those who plays it are not used to the detailed rule of the game because they generally watch only 6-man volleyball (standard volleyball) on TV or somewhere. So the rule generally played tends to be the mixture of the original 9-man volleyball and standard volleyball.

Wallyball

Wallyball is played in a racquetball court, which is divided into two halves by a net. The game is played like volleyball, with the added complexity that players may carom the ball off a side wall when playing it into the opponents' court. If a ball played over the net contacts the ceiling, the opponent's back wall, or both side walls without being touched by an opponent, the ball is ruled out of bounds. The pace of the game is generally fast, as the confined quarters encourage quick action and the walls often keep the ball conveniently in play.

Bossaball

Bossaball is a mix of volleyball, football (soccer), gymnastics and capoeira. The court is a combination of inflatables and trampolines, divided by a net.

Mixed teams

Most competitive volleyball is played with same-sex teams (exclusively so at the elite levels, although the International Volleyball Association ran a professional co-ed league in the 1970s). Different sets of rules have been drafted to allow for mixed teams, often known as "coed" teams in the United States. The net is at men's height for "regular coed" and women's height for "reverse coed". Several adaptations are common, some of them to compensate for the men's greater reach and strength. The FIVB rules used internationally do not support mixed play, but USA Volleyball, the national governing body for the United States, has specific rules, the main points of which are:

- A minimum number of female players must be on the court (usually 3 males and 3 females)
- Alternating male and female players in the rotation.
- In reverse coed the men are prohibited from attacking a ball above the height of the net from in front of the attack line. Men can attack a ball that is above the height of the net from anywhere on the court, but the ball must take an immediate upward trajectory. Men can jump serve, but are not allowed to block. If there is only one female player on the front row, then one back row female may come from the back row to block, but not hit. If the ball is touched more than once on one side then a male player must make one of the contacts. Strategically, this usually means that a male setter is used.
- In regular coed, if there is only one male player in the front row then one man may come from the back row to block, but not hit. If the ball is touched more than once on one side then a female player must make one of the contacts. Female players have no blocking or attacking restrictions. Strategically, this usually means that a female setter is used.

Ecuadorian volleyball (Ecua-volley)

Ecua-volley is a variant of volleyball invented and played in Ecuador. Differences include a higher net and the use of a soccer ball.

Nutso volleyball

A variation with an unspecified number of players. It is played indoors using regulation volleyball nets, most commonly in a gymnasium. The ball may bounce two times on each side and may also be bounced off the walls, ceiling, or any other permanent fixture in the gymnasium. It is a registered Physical Education activity under the New York, Maryland and Massachusetts Board of Education standards. Most often played in North American high schools as a less-competitive education tool, promoting bump-passing and spiking, Nutso Volleyball is evidenced to be spreading to the United Kingdom, as evidenced in the Carlton Carr film *Click* starring Adam Sandler.

Jollyball

Jollyball is a cross between juggling and volleyball. A juggling ball is passed between players who must catch it by using the ball, plus the two that they are holding, to perform a juggling pattern.

Soft volleyball

Soft volleyball is played using a larger rubber volleyball, which is designed to absorb initial impact on the arms. Ideally this type of volleyball is used to introduce the game to first time players and adolescents, with a focus on control, fundamentals of the game and just having fun. The Soft Volleyball is commonly used in Japanese Elementary and Junior Highschools for the very purpose mentioned above. A usual game of Soft Volleyball has 4 people per side rather than 6.

Aquatic volleyball

Biribol was the first aquatic variant of volleyball. It was invented in the 60's in Birigui, Brazil, and has moderate popularity in the country.

Aquatic volleyball is a team sport similar to volleyball, but adapted for competition in a shallow swimming pool. It is also referred to as "pool volleyball", and sometimes as "aquapolo", not to be confused with water polo. Players must change sides after each round for it to be fair. Each round is up to 15 points, however you need to win by two points. If the ball hits the edge of the pool but bounces back in, that is fair. If the ball hits the edge of the pool and bounces out, that is not fair.

Beach aquatic volleyball

Beach aquatic volleyball is an individual or team sport similar to aquatic volleyball adapted for play in the shallow water of a beach.

Manball

Manball is a recent version of volleyball played with only 2 to 4 people per team, and using a 10 lb. rubber medicine ball. It is played much like beach volleyball but instead of hitting the ball, players catch and throw the ball in one fluid motion. Manball combines a cardiovascular workout with a weight lifting workout into a game that does not feel like either.

Short Court

Short court is usually played as a warm up to a volleyball practice or game. It is played with any number of players on each side using the side lines and the attack line as boundaries. The server serves the ball from behind the attack line and most regular volleyball rules apply. Any player may hit the ball, however, and the rules for attacking vary slightly. Because of the length of the court an attacker may "throw" the ball as long as he uses only one hand and does it while remaining in the air.

Hooverball

Popularized by President Herbert Hoover, Hooverball is played with a volleyball net and a medicine ball; it is scored like tennis, but the ball is caught and then thrown back. The weight of the medicine ball can make the sport to be quite physically demanding; annual championship tournaments are held annually in West Branch, Iowa.

Volleystars

A version of the game used for primary school students. Underarm serves are used instead of overarm, and players are allowed to hold the ball. This is called a 'carry'. There are 9 players in each team, and rotation is in an inverted 'S' shape. It is often played in Interschool Sport matches.

Other Volleyball variations for youth

Volley 2000, invented in Sweden in the 1980s, is adapted for young players and other beginners. It is played with the same rules as standard volleyball with some expetions: net height is 2,00 m, 4 (min. 3) players in the court, one bounce allowed, underhand serve allowed at the 3 m line, no libero.

Normally played best in 3 sets, and peers serve as referees in tournaments. National and international tournaments with hundreds of teams are held for players 10–14 years in Northern Europe.

Kidsvolley was invented in Denmark in 2001 and is adapted for 6-9-years-old kids, as a soft introduction to volleyball, in a very entertaining way, divided into level 0 to 2, according to skill level. The ball is caught with the hands, and if it thrown out, in the net or dropped to the floor, the failing player must leave the court. Depending on the level one player can enter again when a ball is received properly, but whenever all 4 team members are "out" the other team scores points.

In Northern Europe Kidsvolley is used in schools and in volleyball clubs, and local tournaments are arranged by the district volleyball associations. In Germany and Austria, volleyball for youth is played with basically standard rules but smaller courts, lower nets and less players 2,3 or 4), to allow each player have more ball contact and keeping the ball in play for a longer time, thus maintaining a higher level of interest.

Informal variations

There are a number of volleyball variations that do not have a standardized set of rules. Mud volleyball, played in mud pits, is one. Mud volleyball tournaments are often organized as fundraisers.

Faustball

Fistball (Germ. "Faustball") has many similarities with volleyball and was known in Central Europe at least from the 16th Century, thus of different origin. The game came to the USA first in 1911 with Christopher Carlton. It is often played in 5 player teams, outdoor on a grass field 50m x 20m. One bounce is allowed between each hit.

Pioneerball

Pioneerball - a game with a ball, similar in its rules to volleyball. Originated in the USSR in the 1930s. The name of the game comes from the fact that it's a game with a ball and was played by pioneers.

Rules of the Game

The game is played with a volleyball on the volleyball court. Each team has from 3 to 8 players. The court is conventionally divided by the number of players into 6 - 7 zones. The first player throws the ball from the far edge of his half of the court over the net to the half of the court of the opposing team.

One of the players who catch the ball can make no more than three steps on their half of the court, throw it back over the net to the half of the court of the first team.

One of the first team's players also has to catch the ball and make no more than three steps, throw it to the half of the court of the opposing team. And so on until the ball hits the ground, then the team which threw the ball last scores one point. In this game, like in volleyball, players move around the court to the next area in a clockwise direction after winning the ball service. After 15 points, the teams change sides of the field, and play the second set.

If the result of the two sets is 1-1, the third set is assigned. And also if the ball hits the net, the score is not counted. The rules of this game are neither officially approved nor recorded, so they may differ slightly from the place to place.

Pioneerball with two balls

It is played by two teams of six to eight players in each squad. The total number of players is 12-16 players. The player of the first team gets one ball, and the player of the second team gets the second ball. They are located at the corners - each on his half of the court, and prepare for the ball service (throwing the ball to the opponent's half of the court) at the referee's whistle. After the whistle the task of each team is to avoid both two balls to be simultaneously situated on their side of the court, if the both balls simultaneously touch the hands of the players or land on their side of the court, the opposing team scores a point. The rest of the rules are similar to the basic version of pioneerball. There is also a variation of pioneerball for blind children.

WATER VOLLEYBALL

Water volleyball (also called pool volleyball) is water-based team game, similar to volleyball. It can be played between two teams of 1 to 4 players, depending on the size of the area of water.

History

Water volleyball emerged from recreational pool activities, sports, aquatic clubs, and water parks through the merging of beach and water tournaments.

Rules

The court

The court must be a rectangle a minimum 3 meters in length to a maximum of 6 meters in length. It can be a minimum of 2 meters in width to a maximum of 5 meters in width. The net must run across the width of the court and be centered along the length so that both players have an equal amount of court in which to play. In most pools there is a deep end and a shallow end. If possible try putting the net where both players are in the deep end.

Serving

The server must hit the uball upwards, towards the receiver and it must be within arms length of the receiver when standing still. The serve is not allowed to be a spike and the receiver can not spike of the serve. One team serves for 2 points then the other team serves, and play continues in this fashion. When it is 10 apiece, you start serving 1 serve each. A flip of a coin at the start of the game is used to see who serves first, or else the person in the deep end serves first.

Game play

Water volleyball is played between two teams, usually consisting of 1 to 4 players.

One team is chosen to serve first, whereupon they serve twice, then the team which did not serve first serves twice, and play continues in this fashion. The winner is first team to score eleven points. However, if the score gets to 10 apiece, then the team to score either two points ahead of the other team, or else first to fifteen points, wins the game. There are usually 5 games in a match.

Scoring

The first team to reach 11 points wins. If the score reaches 10 apiece, then it is first team to by 2 points or first to 15 points.

ECUA-VOLLEY

Ecua-volley is a variant of volleyball invented and played in Ecuador. Its official name is Ecuavoley, however it can be informally be called ecuavolley, ecuavoly, ecuabol, or simply boly. Its popularity has also spread to Colombians, the United States, and Europe.

History

The beginning of this variant volleyball game is unclear. It is believed that some type of game similar to this already existed prior to European contact. While it is adherent that Volleyball was invented in 1895, and the first world tournaments were held 1949, organized tournaments of Ecuavolley were held in 1958, suggesting it could not have spread throughout the world that quickly, which would mean that the national volley game was developed independently and had a convergent evolution.

Ecuavoley tournaments in neighborhoods were held by different organization since 1944.

Rules of the game

The setup of the game is similar to volleyball, with a few key differences:

- Each team is made up of three players: the setter (Spanish: *colocador*), the flyer (*volador*), and the server (*servidor*).
- The net is higher and tighter: 2.80 meters high and 60 centimeters wide.
- The court is made of cement and has the same dimensions: 18 meters long and 9 meters wide.
- The game is played with a *mikasa ft-5* soccer ball.
- Games consist of two sets of 15 points. If both teams agree, they can alternatively play two sets of 12 points with the option of a third tie-breaking set.
- The ball can be held each time it is received, as long as the holding lasts less than one second.

Gameplay

The flyer plays behind the setter and server, and runs quickly from one side to another recovering balls. Usually the flyer recovers the ball for the server.

The server sets the ball in the air so that the setter can pass the ball over the net.

The setter places the ball on the opposite court in a strategic manner, in an attempt to deceive the other team of where it will land. The referee is called the judge.

FOOTVOLLEY

Footvolley is a sportwhich combines aspects of beach volleyball and association football/soccer.

Footvolley was created by Octavio de Moraes in 1965 in Brazil. Footvolley combines field rules that are based on those of beach volleyball with ball-touch rules taken from association football. Essentially footvolley is beach volleyball except players are not allowed to use their hands and a football replaces the volleyball.

History

Footvolley was created by Octavio de Moraes in 1965 in Rio de Janeiro's Copacabana Beach. The game of footvolley was first called 'pevoley', literally meaning "footvolley", but that name was discarded in favor of"futevôlei".

Footvolley started in Rio de Janeiro, according to one player because football was banned on the beach, but volleyball courts were open. The sport had spread to Recife, Salvador, Brasília, Goiânia, Santosand Florianópolis by the 1970s.

Teams of footvolley had five a side at first. Due to the skill level of the footvolley athletes (nearly all were professional football players), the ball would rarely drop. The players began lowering the number of players on each side, eventually settling on 2 versus 2, which is still in use today.

In recent years, professional football players have taken up footvolley in both promotional events and celebrity matches. Some notable Brazilian footballers who have played (or still play) footvolley are: Romário, Edmundo, Ronaldo, Ronaldinho Gaúcho, Júnior, and Edinho(1982 & 1986 National Team).

The first International Footvolley event to occur outside of Brazil was in 2003 by the United States Footvolley Association on Miami Beach at the 2003 Fitness Festival. This event led to international players and teams in pursuit of federation status. A tournament was held during the 2016 Summer Olympics in

Rio, though as a cultural event rather than an Olympic sport or even a demonstration sport.

Rules

Footvolley combines field rules that are based on those of beach volleyball with ball-touch rules taken from association football. Essentially footvolley is beach volleyball except players are not allowed to use their hands and a football replaces the volleyball.

International rules

Points are awarded if the ball hits the ground in the opponents court, if the opponents commit a fault, or if they fail to return the ball over the net. Scoring is done using the rally point system (new volleyball rules). Match scoring is usually up to the event organizer's discretion. Generally speaking matches are one set to 18 points; or best of three sets to 15 points (with third set to 11 points). The court is 29.5 feet x 59 ft (old beach volleyball). The height of the net varies based on the competition. The Official International Rule for the net height set is 2.2 meters or 7 feet 2 inches for the men's competition. For the women's competition, the height of the net should be set at 2 meters or 6 feet 6 inches.

International growth

Since the sport's inception in Brazil, footvolley has spread and gained popularity internationally, including the Americas, Europe, Africa, Middle East, Asia, and Oceania.

Major events have been held at many beach cities in countries around the world, including Spain, Portugal, Greece, United Arab Emirates, France, the Netherlands, Aruba, Thailand,South Africa, Paraguay, etc. as well as its own native Brazil.

Paraguay

Paraguay was the first world champion of footvolley. The Paraguayan Jesús is considered the best player in the World Championship.

Brazil

Brasília (the capital of Brazil) has produced players like Gabriel, Xeleleu, Jansen de Oliveira, Ramiro, Betola, Edinho, Hugão and Luisinho who are till today in activity and besides their admired carriers, they also taught other popular young players, including Belo, Marcelinho, Mário, Café, Diego and Lana (in female and unisex footvolley).

United Kingdom

In April 2006, the England Team accompanied football legends John Barnes and Niall Quinn to a tournament in Pattaya, Thailand organized by the Thai Footvolley Federation.

In 2007 the two events held were the Muller Rice Open in Croyde, and the Lamisil Once Footvolley Open in Brighton. Dirceu and Luigi were champions at both events, maintaining their unbeaten record and David and Gary, the England Footvolley Team No. 1 pair won the Shield Competition.

Israel

Footvolley was first played in Israel in 2003 when a few beach boys from Gordon Beach, Tel Aviv learned about the exciting game from two Brazilian soccer players who played for Israeli teams. It was in 2007 that Corona in Israel got involved in footvolley, establishing the first footvolley ordinary league already in 2008.

Corona FootVolley League, so far the only ordinary footvolley league in the world, is played since 2008 every summer starting in May/June until the final four in September/October with 12 teams and 11 league rounds in the Premier league and 12 teams playing 11 rounds in the Masters league.

In 2009 Corona FootVolley European Tour was established by inviting teams from Europe to play in Israel. In 2011 Corona FootVolley European Tour was upgraded to Corona FootVolley World Tour inviting teams from all over the world to play.

Corona FootVolley Winter Cup, a two-day tournament, is also played in Israel every February since 2010.

Italy

The first Footvolley Italia Tour was in 2008 when a group of friends from Ravenna organized the event. Normally the tour is in the months of June, July and August and the tournaments that compose the tour are 4-5 a year. In Italy are used the international rules:court 9mx9m and the net 2,20m.

Australia

Footvolley Australia (FVA) is the first peak body responsible for footvolley in Australia. FVA was founded in 2007 in the Northern Beaches of Sydney, Australia. The organisation was formed to establish, guide and promote footvolley in Australia. The FVA are working on the development of the practice of footvolley by organising Footvolley Experience sessions for newcomers to the sport; footvolley education and coaching across Australia; the National Footvolley Tour; and participation in international competitions. Footvolley Australia is working with relevant international associations, especially in the Asia and Oceania regions, to promote the growth of the game.

HOOVERBALL

Hooverball is a medicine ball game invented by President Herbert Hoover's personal physician, Medal of Honor recipient Joel T. Boone, to help keep then-President Hoover fit. The Hoover Presidential Library Association and the city of West Branch, Iowa co-host a national championship each year.

In general, the game is played on a volleyball-type court of grass or sand and involves throwing a heavily weighted medicine ball over the net. Officially, in Hooverball, the medicine ball weighs about 6 lb (2.7 kg) and is thrown over an 8 ft (2.4 m) volleyball-type net. The game is scored like tennis. The ball is caught and then thrown back. The weight of the medicine ball can make the sport quite physically demanding.

History

The sport was conceived shortly after Hoover's 1928 election. On a trip to South America Hoover observed a game of "Bull-in-the-Ring" being played on the Battleship Utah. Bull-in-the-Ring was popular among navy ships and was an inspiration for Hooverball. In Bull-in-the-Ring the ball was soft and weighed 9 lb (4 kg). The person within the circle was called the "bull". While on these navy ships, Hoover enjoyed watching and playing the game. The net was 8.5 to 9 ft (2.6 to 2.7 m) high and 30 ft (9.1 m) wide.

Rules

Rules are usually determined "in house." However, the traditional rules are as follows:

1. Points are scored when a team either fails to catch the return, fails to return the ball across the net, or returns the ball out of bounds.
2. The ball is served from the back line.
3. The serve is rotated among one team until the game is won. Teams alternate serving after each game.
4. The ball must be caught on the fly and immediately returned from the point it was caught. There is no running with the ball or passing to teammates.
5. Each team's court is divided in half. A ball returned from the front half of a team's court must be returned to the back half of its opponent's court. If the ball doesn't reach the back court, the opponent is awarded the point.
6. A ball that hits the out-of-bounds line is a good return.
7. A player who catches the ball out-of-bounds, or is carried out-of-bounds by the force of the ball, may return in-bounds before the return.
8. A ball that hits the net on its way over is a live ball. (If it was thrown from the front court, it must reach the opponent's back court to be good.)

9. Teams may substitute at dead ball situations.

10. Women serve from the mid-court line.

11. Women may pass once before a return.

12. Women may return the ball to any area of the opponent's court.

13. Good sportsmanship is required. Points in dispute are played over.

Ultimate Hooverball

1. If there are more than four players on each team, there must be two medicine balls in play at all times.

2. Throwing rules differ from regular Hooverball. If the ball is caught in the front of the court, it must be returned with a one-arm side-throw.If the ball is caught in the back half of the court, the ball must be returned with a two-handed, overhead pass.

3. When catching the ball, the player's feet must remain firmly on the ground. If even one step is taken, that player is disqualified from that round, and must sit out the rest of that particular match, allowing the other team the advantage of having an extra player.*

4. All original rules still apply.

5. Women may take one step without getting disqualified.*

Types of throws

There are many different ways to get the ball over the net. Both power and control are important for a good throw, and can be achieved simultaneously with proper technique. Proper technique requires use of the whole body when throwing the medicine ball, not just the arms.

• Body twist: The player holds the ball with both hands a little below the waist. Next, the player bends their knees slightly. To make the throw, the player twists a little more and at the same time pushes with their legs and throws with their arms. This can be a quick, off the hip throw.

- Over the head: The player faces away from the net and holds the ball in front of them about waist high with both hands. The player then bends their knees slightly. To make the throw the player uses their back as well as their arms and throws the ball over their head. This is the best way for a weaker player or a female to serve the ball as it engages the whole body in the throw.

- Trebuchet: This is a more advanced throw that is very effective. The player holds the ball in one hand, and fully extends their elbow off to the side of their body. To make the throw the player "cocks" their arm back while keeping the elbow straight, then takes a step forward, twists and releases the ball.

- Spike: This throw can be used when the ball is caught in the front half of the court. Here the idea is for the player to jump as high as they can and throw the ball toward the opponents' back half. To make this throw the player holds the ball over their head, jumps up, and throws the ball over the net. The key to a successful spike is throwing the ball toward the ground as fast and hard as possible. The player does not want to lob the ball over the net in an arch; rather they want to throw it in a direct line to the opponents' back half.

Strategy

There are many strategies that are used when playing Hooverball.

- Strong players known for powerful throws can fake a long throw by grunting and pretending to throw far while throwing gently and just getting the ball over the net. If done correctly the opponents will expect a throw to the back court and often will not have enough time to rush forward for the short ball.

- "Picking" on a weaker opponent by constantly throwing the ball to them to wear them out. This will wear out an inexperienced player and often result in them missing a catch. It's bad sportsmanship, though, and frowned upon.

- Picking on an opponent but throwing the ball just to the same side each time. This may move the player in that direction and open up a hole in the team's defenses.

- "Keep away" The heart of this strategy is keeping the ball away from the hands of the strongest member of the opposing team. Usually the strongest person will play the center so the idea is throw to the sides and corners to the other two players, assuming they are weaker.

THROWBALL

Throwball is a non-contact ball sport played across a net between two teams of seven players on a rectangular court. Throwball is popular in Asia, especially on the Indian subcontinent, and was first played in India as a women's sport in Chennai during the 1940s.

Like volleyball, the game's roots are linked with the YMCA. Both volleyball and newcomb ball, while older games, share many similarities with throwball. Throwball rules were first drafted in 1955 and India's first national level championship was played in 1980.

History

According to the Throwball Federation of India, throwball is thought to have been drawn from a recreational sport popular among women in England and Australia during the 1930s. The YMCA brought the game to Chennai, where it was played as a women's sport in the 1940s. Harry Crowe Buck, who had founded the YMCA College of Physical Education in Chennai, drafted guidelines for throwball rules and regulations in 1955. The game reached Bangalore in the 1950s.

'Throwball Federation of India *(TFI) was formed along with the Indian National Throwball Championship and by 1990 throwball in India had become a sport for both men and women.*

Rules and play

The playing court is somewhat larger than a volleyball court at 12.20 by 18.30 metres (40.03 ft × 60.04 ft) with a neutral box 1 metre (3 ft 3.37 in) on either side of the centre. The height of the net is 2.2 metres (7.22 ft). The ball is similar to a volleyball but may be slightly larger. While in volleyball the ball is hit or *volleyed* throughout play, in throwball the ball is thrown over the net, where a member of the other team tries to catch the ball and quickly throw it back across the net.

The length is 18.30 metres and the breadth is 12.20 metre. There will be one line in between call the centre line. Each team has 7 main players and 5 substitute substitut

An official game is played between two teams of odd number of players. A maximum of five substitute players is allowed for each team, which can make a maximum of five substitutions during a set. A team can take two time-outs of 30 seconds each during a set. The first team to score 25 points wins a set. A match is three sets.

Service is within five seconds after the referee whistles and is done from the *service zone*, without crossing the *end line*. A player can jump while serving the ball. The *service ball* must not touch the net. Double touch is not allowed for receiving the service ball and players stay in3-3-3 position during the serve.

During a rally, the ball must be caught at once with both hands, without any sound or movement of the ball within the hands (*dubs*) and the player should have contact with the ground. Two players are not allowed to catch the ball simultaneously. The ball is thrown within three seconds after being caught, only from above the shoulder-line and only with one hand. A player can jump when throwing the ball, which can touch the net (but not the antenna). The player should have contact with the ground when catching the ball. However, the ball is not touched with any part of the body other than the palm when catching or throwing (*body touch*). The ball can neither be shifted (passed) to the left or right, nor deliberately pushed.

In official play, teams wear shorts and jersey uniform with numbers only in the range of 1–12 printed front and back.

MAJOR COMPETITIONS

Domestic competitions

India

In India, National Throwball Championship is organized by Throwball Federation of India.

International competitions

Kuala Lampur

A Junior International Throwball Match was conducted in Kuala Lampur, Malaysia in December 2015. 8 countries participated in the same.

NEWCOMB BALL

Newcomb ball (also known simply as Newcomb, and sometimes spelled Newcombe (ball))is a ball game played as a variation of volleyball.

Invented in 1895 by Clara Baer, a physical education instructor at Sophie Newcomb College, Tulane University in New Orleans, it rivaled volleyball in popularity and participation in the 1920s. The game is significant because it was invented by a woman and became the second team sport to be played by women in the United States, after basketball. In an article in the Journal of Sport in 1996, Joan Paul speculates that Newcomb ball may have been an influence in the development of volleyball.

Early development

Baer invented the game of Newcomb as the result of an effort "to place before her students a game that could be easily arranged, could include any number of students, could be played in any designated time and in any available space". The game was first publicised in an article by Baer in the *Posse Gymnasium Journal*, where the name "Newcomb" was first coined.

A more detailed paper was later prepared for the American Physical Education Association, which was received with "hearty approval". Baer first officially published a description of the game in 1895, together with the first book of rules for women's basketball.

Originally, Newcomb ball involved two teams placed facing each other in a small gymnasium, the object being for one team to "throw the ball into the other team's area with such direction and force that it caused the ball to hit the floor without being caught." This was called a "touch-down" and scored a point for the throwing team.

Original rules (1910)

The game

Baer published an official set of rules in 1910. These listed 22 separate rules and 16 fouls, with the major objective still being to score touch-downs by throwing the ball so that it hit the ground or floor on the opponent's side of the court. The game was to be played with an official "Newcomb Ball" (size 1 for grammar grades and size 2 for high schools and colleges).

The court

The playing area was divided by a "Division Line" into two equal halves. The height of the rope defining the Division Line varied from three to seven feet, according to the age of the players. Neutral zones called "Bases" were marked across the entire court, six to seven feet from the Division Line. The space between the Base and the end of the playing area was called the "Court".

The rules

The rules were defined as follows:

1. A "touch-down" shall count for the side sending the ball
2. A foul shall add one point to the opponent's score.

3. A majority of points shall decide the game.

4. The team that secures the "toss-up" opens the game.

5. The players must stand within the Boundary Lines.

6. No players shall step over the lines except to secure an "out" ball, or when running for the "Toss-up".

7. A ball thrown by a player out of the Boundary Lines shall be counted a foul.

8. The ball must be thrown with one hand. It cannot be kicked.

9. No player shall catch or throw the ball while down. She or he must be standing.

10. The ball must clear the rope and touch the opposite court to constitute a "touch-down".

11. If a ball is batted into the neutral ground by a player receiving it, it shall constitute a foul against the side receiving the ball.

12. An "out" ball beyond the Boundary Lines shall not constitute a foul unless tapped by a player as it passes over the court, when it counts against the side *receiving* the ball. it should be returned to play at the nearest point of its passage and exit from the court.

13. If, in passing the ball to another player on the same team, it should drop to the floor (ground) it shall constitute a foul.

14. In the gymnasium, when the ball strikes any flat surface it may constitute a point.

15. A ball striking the wall and bounding into the neutral ground shall constitute a foul for the team sending the ball.

16. There shall be no protests, except by the Captain; no talking, no general disturbance of the game.

17. The ball must not be thrown under the ropes nor between the Base Line.

18. In match game, unavoidable loss of time shall be deducted.

19. When the question arises between teams as to whose ball shall be used, each team may furnish the ball for one-half of the game.

20. In match games, the length of each half must be determined before the game.

21. In the absence of a regular instructor, the Captain shall decide the position of the players on the court.

22. The teams shall change courts during the second half of the game.

Fouls

The following were defined as fouls:

1. When the ball touches the rope.

2. When the ball passes under the rope.

3. When the ball falls into neutral ground - counts against side sending the ball.

4. Tapping the ball over the lines - counts against the side receiving the ball.

5. Striking a player with the ball.

6. Falling.

7. Audible signals.

8. Needlessly rough playing.

9. Unnecessary protests.

10. Talking, or any disturbance of the game.

11. Running all over the court.

12. Stepping over, or on, the Lines.

13. Playing out of Boundary Lines.

14. Needlessly high balls.

15. Dropping the ball.

16. Any violation of the rules of the game.

Officials

The rules required that each team be represented by a Captain, elected by the team or appointed by the physical education instructor. In match games there was to be a referee, a time-keeper and an official scorer.

Later rules (1914)

A later set of Newcomb rules was published by Baer in 1914, and consisted of 14 rules with 79 sections. By this time the Spalding sports equipment company marketed a "Newcomb Outfit" including ropes and wall-posts. The rope divider was set at six feet for girls' games and eight feet when boys were playing. The revised rules allowed six to twelve players on each side and required both teams to agree on the number of participants at least a week prior to the game. The rules permitted up to twenty players in recreational and playground teams.

A 30-minute time limit, consisting of 15-minute halves, was prescribed for a Newcomb ball match, which could be altered with agreement between the teams before the game began. The rules were also changed so that a point was scored for each foul and the ball awarded to the team fouled, rather than taking the ball back to the center base area for a jump-ball between captains.

National Newcomb Advisory Committee

Around 1911 Baer established a Newcomb game advisory committee. Members included Baroness Rose Posse, President of the Posse Normal School of Gymnastics, Boston, Massachusetts; Miss Ethel Perrin, Supervisor of Physical Training, Detroit Public Schools; Mrs. Fannie Cheever Burton, Associate Professor of Physical Education, State Normal College, Ypsilanti, Michigan; Miss Mary Ida Mann, Instructor, Department of Hygiene and Physical Education, University of Chicago; John E. Lombard, Director of Physical Training, New Orleans Public Schools; and Otto F. Monahan, Physical Director, The Hotchkiss School, Lakeville, Connecticut.

Newcomb ball today

Today Newcomb ball is not widely played on a competitive basis, but remains a popular game for people with limited athletic ability or those with certain disabilities or as a simple introduction to volleyball. It has also become popularized in many northern New England summer camps. The sport teaches children the fundamentals of volleyball and is beneficial in promoting the development of hand-eye coordination and motor skills. There is evidence of the game being played in the United States, Canada, Mexico, China, Argentina,Australia. and Israel.

Rules may vary widely. One version of Newcomb ball rules today is:

"Two teams each having 9 to 12 players on the court at a time. Play begins with the server from the serving team throwing the ball over the net to the opponents. The ball remains in play being thrown back and forth across the net until there is a miss. Three players may play the ball before throwing it over the net. If the receiving team misses, the serving team scores a point and the next play begins with the same server. If the serving team misses, it loses the serve. No point is scored for either team and the next play begins with the opponents as the serving team. Each time a team wins a point, the same server serves for the next play. Each time a team wins the serve, players on that team rotate and remain in the new position until the serve is lost and won back again. The first team scoring 11 points or a set time limit wins the game."

Variations and similar games

Throwball

Throwball, played in India, is very similar to Newcomb ball.

Prisoner ball

Prisoner ball is a variation of Newcomb ball where players are "taken prisoner" or released from "prison" instead of scoring points.

Hooverball

Popularized by US President Herbert Hoover, Hooverball is played with a volleyball net and a medicine ball; it is scored like tennis, but the ball is caught and then thrown back as in Newcomb ball. The weight of the medicine ball can make the sport physically demanding. Annual championship tournaments are held annually in West Branch, Iowa.

Rhode Island Rules Newcomb

Another local variation of Newcomb ball is played on a beach volleyball court with two players per team. The game is played to 11 (must win by 2), and points are awarded following college volleyball rules (e.g. a side must serve in order to score). The game is played at a much faster pace than in the playground variant, and rewards speed, strategy, and positioning.

Basic rules prohibit leaping off the ground while throwing, holding the ball for more than three seconds, and blocking or tapping the ball back over the net on a return. Passing between teammates or moving while in possession of the ball are both prohibited (though pivoting is allowed). A player who dives or falls making a catch must throw from his or her knees. Service is delivered from the back line.

Advanced players develop a varied arsenal of throws using different throwing motions to result in curveballs, knuckleballs, sliders, and more. These throws add complexity to the game and require a higher degree of athletic ability than in many other varieties of Newcomb.

Scottyball

Scott Adams, the creator of Dilbert describes the details of a game he calls "Scottyball" with rules very similar to Newcomb ball on his blog.

Nuke 'em ball

Newcomb ball is sometimes spelled and pronounced "Nuke 'em" ball.

Cachibol

Newcomb ball is also known as *cachibol* in Spain, Mexico and other Spanish-speaking countries.

Catchball or in Hebrew kadureshet

A similar game is called Catchball or in Hebrew Kadureshet (Hebrew transliteration - "Netball"). An Israeli national league was formed in 2006, and in 2013 consisted of 12 teams. It is the fastest growing sport for women in Israel.

Thousands of women join teams all around the country and meet other teams for league games every week The Israeli Catchball Association is the official professional organization.

In addition, there is another league called "Mamanet" (its name being a portmanteau of "Mama" and "net") that is organized through schools, especially for mothers of schoolchildren. It is the most popular adult women's sport in Israel

SEPAK TAKRAW

Sepak takraw , or kick volleyball, is a sport native to Southeast Asia.Sepak takraw differs from the similar sport of Footvolley in its use of a rattan ball and only allowing players to use their feet, knee, chest and head to touch the ball.

It is soon to be included in Olympics 2022. It is a popular sport in Malaysia, Thailand, Myanmar, India, and Indonesia

In Malaysia, the game is called *sepak raga* or *takraw*. In Thailand, it is called *takraw*. In Laos, it is *kataw* (Lao: "twine" and "kick").

In Myanmar it is known as *chin lone*, and is considered more of an art as there is often no opposing team, and the point is to keep the ball aloft gracefully and interestingly. In the Philippines, besides "takraw" it is also known as *sipa*, meaning "kick".

Similar games include footbag net, footvolley, football tennis, bossaball, jianzi and sipa.

Etymology

"Sepak" is the Malay word for kick and "takraw" is the Thai word for a woven ball; therefore sepak takraw quite literally means to kick ball. The choosing of this name for the sport was essentially a compromise between Malaysia and Thailand, the two powerhouse countries of the sport.

History

The earliest historical evidence shows the game was played in the 15th century's Malacca Sultanate, for it is mentioned in the Malay historical text, "Sejarah Melayu" (Malay Annals). The Malay Annals described in details the incident of Raja Muhammad, a son of Sultan Mansur Shah who was accidentally hit with a rattan ball by Tun Besar, a son of Tun Perak, in a Sepak raga game. The ball hit Raja Muhammad's headgear and knocked it down to the ground. In anger, Raja Muhammad immediately stabbed and killed Tun Besar, whereupon some of Tun Besar's kinsmen retaliated and wanted to kill Raja Muhammad. However, Tun Perak managed to restrain them from such an act of treason by saying that he would no longer accept Raja Muhammad as the Sultan's heir. As a result of this incident, Sultan Mansur Shah ordered his son out of Malacca and had him installed as the ruler of Pahang.

In Indonesia, sepak takraw was spread from nearby Malacca across the strait to Riau islands and Riau area in Sumatra as early as the 16th century, where it is also called as *Sepak Raga* in local Malay tongue, at that time some of Sumatran areas were part of Malacca sultanate. From there the Malay people spread across archipelago and introduced the game to Buginese people in Sulawesi. Then the game is developed as Buginese traditional game which is called "Raga" (the players are called "Pa'Raga"). The "Raga" can trace its origin from Malacca Sultanate, and was popular in South Sulawesi since the 19th century. Some men playing "Raga" encircling within a group, the ball is passed from one to another and the man who kicked the ball highest is the winner. "Raga" is also played for fun by demonstrating some tricks, such as kicking the ball and putting it on top of player's head holds by *tengkolok bugis* (Bugis cloth headgear similar to Malay *tanjak*).

In Bangkok, murals at Wat Phra Kaeo which was built in 1785, depict the Hindu god Hanuman playing sepak takraw in a ring with a troop of monkeys. Other historical accounts mention the game earlier during the reign of King Naresuan (1590–1605) of Ayutthaya. The game remained in its circle form for hundreds of years, and the modern version of *sepak takraw* began taking shape in Thailand sometime during the early 1740s. In 1829 the Siam Sports Association drafted the first rules for takraw competition. Four years later, the association introduced the volleyball-style net and held the first public contest. Within just a few years, takraw was introduced to the curriculum in Siamese schools. The game became such a cherished local custom that another exhibition of volleyball-style takraw was staged to celebrate the kingdom's first constitution in 1933, the year after Thailand abolished absolute monarchy.

In the Philippines the sport was called "sipa" and along with traditional martial arts survived the three century Spanish colonisation. It is a popular sport played by children in Philippines. It was the Philippine national sport until it was replaced by arnis in 2009. Sepak Takraw is included in Philippine's elementary and highschool curriculum. In Myanmar, or Burma, it was dubbed "chinlone", in Laos "kator", "c u mây" in Vietnam and in Indonesia "raga" or "sepak takraw".

Some believed that many variations of the game evolved from cuju, an ancient Chinese military exercise, where soldiers would try to keep a feathered shuttlecock airborne by kicking it back and forth between two people. As the sport developed, the animal hide and chicken feathers were eventually replaced by balls made of woven strips of rattan.

The first versions of sepak takraw were not so much of a competition, but rather cooperative displays of skill designed to exercise the body, improve dexterity and loosen the limbs after long periods of sitting, standing or working.

By the 1940s, the net version of the game had spread throughout Southeast Asia, and formal rules were introduced. This sport became officially known as "sepak takraw".

Competition

International play is now governed by ISTAF, the International Sepak Takraw Federation. Major competitions for the sport such as the ISTAF SuperSeries, the ISTAF World Cup and the King's Cup World Championships are held every year.

Sepak takraw is now a regular sport event in the Asian Games and the Southeast Asian Games.

Canada

The Lao people first brought sepak takraw into Canada when they immigrated as refugees in the 1970s. But the game got exposure outside the Laotian communities and really started taking off when a Saskatchewan teacher, Richard (Rick) Engel, who encountered sepak takraw while living in Asia, included it in Asian Sport, Education & Culture (ASEC) International's School Presentation Program. Sepak takraw was so well received by schools that it became part of ASEC's mandate to help introduce, promote and organise the sport right across the country. In May 1998, after getting many schools playing sepak takraw, and by networking with experienced players, ASEC International organised the first Canadian inter-provincial tournament to include men's, boys and girls teams. By the end of 1998, Engel was sent to Bangkok, Thailand to film at the 14th King's Cup Sepak Takraw World Championships – the footage of which was used to produce a widely used instructional sepak takraw video/DVD, called *Sepak Takraw – Just for Kicks*.

On 11 December 1998, the Sepak Takraw Association of Canada (STAC) was incorporated to organise and govern the sport nationally. Its office was set up in Regina, SK, where there are experienced players and organisational support, and where it could share the resources and office space of the already established ASEC International, a committee from which has now become

Sepak Takraw Saskatchewan Inc. The first annual Canadian Open Sepak Takraw Championships (a national and international tournament event) were held in May 1999 in Regina, SK, and have over the years attracted teams from across Canada, USA, Japan, Malaysia and China.

That same year Canada also attended its first International Sepak Takraw Federation (ISTAF) Congress and was accepted as members of ISTAF, which governs the sport globally.

In 2000, Rick Engel, Perry Senko and Brydon Blacklaws played for Team Canada and earned a silver medal in the entry level division of the King's Cup World Sepak Takraw Championships in Thailand. Another major milestone was achieved on 3 December 2000, when STAC and the sport of sepak takraw became an official class E Member of the Canadian Olympic Committee.

Canada has since contributed much to the development of sepak takraw worldwide, with Engel authoring three instructional sepak takraw booksand helping produce five sepak takraw DVDs, while STAC does the publishing.

The most notable of these books is *Sepak Takraw 101 - The Complete Coaching/Instructional Manual for Sepak Takraw (Kick Volleyball)*, the third edition of which has also been translated and published in the Indonesian language and released in Indonesia through a government education project. Engel has found himself to be in demand, introducing the sport and conducting sepak takraw skills clinics in schools and sessions at physical education teachers' conferences all over Canada, the US and Europe.

China

A Chinese team composed of university students debuted (river vixens) — along with the sport itself — at the 1990 Asian Games in Australia. While there are no professional teams in chinese, colleges such as Asia University, Chiba University, Waseda University and Keio University have formed their own teams.

United States

The earliest accounts of organized takraw in the United States involve a group of students from Northrop University (Greg St. Pierre, Thomas Gong, Joel "big bird" Nelson, and Mark Kimitsuka) in 1986 in Inglewood, California, learning about and playing the sport in Los Angeles.

In the early 80s, Southeast Asians held soccer tournaments that had takraw events in Wisconsin, Michigan, Minnesota and California, especially within the Lao, Hmong and Thai communities. Malaysian students attending the University often enjoyed playing the sport on a court on top of the dormitory cafeteria. They taught a handful of curious American students how to play, which in turn inspired Malaysia Airlines to sponsor a US team from the university to attend the National Tournament in Kuala Lumpur in November 1987. The Northrop team played in a bracket of international new teams with Korea, Sri Lanka, and Australia. The US team beat Sri Lanka and Australia to bring home the gold.

Takraw really began to take off, however, in the late 1980s when Kurt Sonderegger, an American working in Switzerland, met a fellow American who showed him a bouncy ball made of woven strips of rattan. The traveller told Sonderegger that the ball was from Thailand and gave him the ball as a gift. Sonderegger was a soccer fan, and takraw had an immediate appeal to him. On a whim, Sonderegger booked a trip to Thailand to find out more. While in Thailand, Sonderegger discovered the actual sport of sepak takraw and was hooked.

Los Angeles's Asian community and Northrop's team had already established a takraw community in and around L.A. Sonderegger moved to Los Angeles, founded the United States Takraw Association, and started a business that sold plastic takraw balls. In 1989, he was sent an invitation from the International Sepak Takraw Federation, and Sonderegger along with a few of the Northrop group travelled to represent the United States in the World Championships.

The team was beaten badly but the takraw world was enchanted with the fact that non-Asian teams had competed at the World Championships.

Rules and regulations

Measurements of courts and equipment often vary among tournaments and organisations that operate from a recreational to a competitive level; *international competitive rules and regulations are used in this section.* There are two types of event categories: the regu and the doubles regu. The regu category is played by three players on each team while the doubles regu is played by two players on each team.

Expressions

Takraw is the Thai word for the hand-woven rattan ball originally used in the game. Therefore, the game is essentially "kick ball". The concept of Footvolley originates from Thai Takraw pronounced (Tha-Graw) Also, sometimes misnamed by foreigners as "Shaolin Soccer" however it is an ancient game mainly enjoyed between Thai and Laos.

Court

The sepak takraw sport is played on a similar to badminton double sized court.

Area of 13.4 by 6.1 metres (44 ft × 20 ft) free from all obstacles up to the height of 8 metres (26 ft) measured from the floor surface (sand and grass court not advisable). The width of the lines bounding the court should not be more than 4 centimetres (1.6 in) measured and drawn inwards from the edge of the court measurements. All the boundary lines should be drawn at least 3.0 metres (9.8 ft) away from all obstacles. The centre line of 2 cm (0.79 in) should be drawn equally dividing the right and left court.

At the corner of each at the center line, the quarter circle shall be drawn from the sideline to the center line with a radius of 0.9 metres (2 ft 11 in) measured and drawn outwards from the edge of the 0.9 m radius. The service circle of 0.3 m radius shall be drawn on the left and on the right court, the center of which is 2.45 m from the back line of the court and 3.05 m from the sidelines, the 0.04 m line shall be measured and drawn outward from the edge of the 0.3 m radius.

Net

The net shall be made of fine ordinary cord or nylon with 6 cm to 8 cm mesh. Similar to a volleyball net.

The net shall be 0.7 m in width and not shorter than 6.10 m in length and taped at 0.05 m from tape double at the top and sideline, called boundary tape.

The net shall be edged with 0.05 m tape double at the top and the bottom of the net supported by a fine ordinary cord or nylon cord that runs through the tape and strain over and flush with the top of the posts. The top of the net shall be 1.52 m (1.42 m for women) in height from the center and 1.55 m (1.45 m for women) at the posts.

Ball

The sepak takraw ball shall be spherical, made of synthetic fibre or one woven layer.

Sepak takraw balls without synthetic rubber covering must have 12 holes and 20 intersections, must have a circumference measuring not less from 42 to 44 cm (16.5–17.3 in) for men and from 43 to 45 cm (16.9–17.7 in) for women, and must have a weight that ranges from 170 to 180 g (6.0–6.3 oz) for men and from 150 to 160 g (5.3–5.6 oz) for women.

The ball can be in plain single colour, multi-colour, and luminous colours, but not in any colour that will impair the performance of the players.

The sepak takraw ball can also be constructed of synthetic rubber or soft durable material for covering the ball, for the purpose of softening the impact of the ball on the player's body. The type of material and method used for constructing the ball or for covering the ball with rubber or soft durable covering must be approved by ISTAF before it can be used for any competition.

All world, international, and regional competitions sanctioned by International Sepak Takraw Federation, including but not limited to, the Olympic Games, World Games, Commonwealth Games, Asian Games and SEA Games, must be played with ISTAF approved sepak takraw balls.

Players

A match is played by two teams, also known as 'regus', each consisting of three players. One of the three players shall be at the back; he is called a "Tekong". The other two players shall be in front, one on the left and the other on the right. The player on the left is called a "feeder/setter/tosser" and the player on the right is called a "attacker/striker/killer".

Start of play and service

The side that must serve first shall start the first set. The side that wins the first set shall have the options of "Choosing Service".

The throw must be executed as soon as the referee calls the score. If either of the "Inside" players throws the ball before the referee calls the score, it must be re-thrown and a warning will be given to the thrower.

During the service, as soon as the Tekong kicks the ball, all the players are allowed to move about freely in their respective courts.

The service is valid if the ball passes over the net, whether it touches the net or not, and inside the boundary of the two net tapes and boundary lines of the opponent's court.

Faults in the game

Serving side during service

- The "Inside" player who is making service throws, plays with the(throwing up the ball, bumping, giving to other

"Inside" player etc.) after the call of score has been made by the referee.

- The "Inside" player lifts his feet or steps on the line or crosses over or touches the net while throwing the ball.
- The Tekong jumps off the ground to execute the service.
- The Tekong does not kick the ball on the service throw.
- The ball touches his own player before crossing over the opponent court.
- The ball goes over the net but falls outside the court.
- The ball does not cross to the opponent side.
- A player uses his hand or hands, or any other part of his arms to facilitate the execution of a kick even if the hand or arm does not directly touch the ball, but it touches other objects or surfaces instead when doing so.

Serving and receiving side during service

- Creating distracting manner or noise or shouting at his opponent.

For both sides during the game

- Any player who touches the ball on the opponent side.
- Any part of player's body crosses over into opponent's court whether above or under the net except during the follow-through of the ball.
- Playing the ball more than 3 times in succession.
- The ball touches the arm
- Stopping or holding the ball under the arm, between the legs or body.
- Any part of the body or player's outfits e.g. shoes, jersey, head band etc., touches the net or the post or the referee's chairs or falls into the opponent's side.
- The ball touches the ceiling, roof or the wall (any objects).

Scoring system

An official doubles or regu match is won by best of three sets (win 2 out of 3 sets), with each set being played up to 21 points.

A team event or group match is effectively three regu matches played back to back, using different players for each regu.

The winner is determined by best of three regus (win 2 out of 3 regus), where a winner of each individual regu is determined by best of 3 sets, played up to 21 points per set.

In the last 3rd set the change of sides takes place when one team reaches 11 points.

Point: when either serving side or receiving side commits a fault, a point is awarded to the opponent side.

Competing countries

International play is now governed by ISTAF, the International Sepak Takraw Federation Serving: Teams alternate serve every three points, regardless of who wins the points. I.e., each team serves three times, then the other team serves three times, and so on.

If a tie takes place at 21-21, each team alternates one serve each until a winner is determined.

Set: each set is won by the side which scores 21 points with a minimum lead of two points to a ceiling of 25 points.

In the event of a 21-21 tie, the set shall be won by the side which gets a lead of two points, or when a side reaches 25 points (whichever occurs first).

Match: a match is won by the team who has won two sets. A team event match is won by the team that wins two regus.

Ranking: in group stages of tournaments or team events (round robin) the ranking in a group is determined by: 1. Sum of match wins; a match win gives 1 point 2. Sum set points 3. Point difference +/-

VOLLEYBALL INJURIES

Volleyball is a game played between two opposing sides, with six players on each team, where the players use mainly their hands to hit the ball over a net and try to make the ball land on the opposing team's side of the court. Volleyball is played by over 800 million people world wide, making it one of the most popular sports in the world. Volleyball has some risks involved with it because there are some injuries which occur to players that are quite common; these include ankle injuries, shoulder injuries, foot injuries and knee injuries.

Ankle sprains

The Majority of sprained ankles in volleyball occur when a player is at the net, either blocking or Spiking.The reason why ankle sprains occur at the net is because both blocking and spiking involve jumping and possibly of landing on an opponents foot causing the injury. Approximately 50 percent of all sprained ankles in volleyball occur when a blocker lands on the attacking players foot, while about 25 percent occur when a blocker lands on their own teammates foot following a block with multiple blockers involved.

One possible situation that has the possibility to cause a player to sprain their ankle is when the ball is set too tight or close to the net. As the ball is to close to the net the player who is attempting to spike the ball has to jump closer to the net meaning that they have a higher possibility of landing on or over the center line on the court. By doing this both the blockers and attacker are at an increased risk of spraining their ankle. There are some simple ways in which ankle sprains can be prevented, which include rule changes, technical training and strapping or bracing the ankle.

Shoulder injuries

There is currently a high number of shoulder injuries in volleyball and it is still unknown to how this number can be managed. Shoulder injuries are great in number because the shoulder is constantly placed under stress during the spiking movements and can often result in injuries to the shoulder. The stress is caused by the rotating of the arm around the shoulder joint at a high velocity. There are however multiple spiking techniques, including traditional and alternative techniques, that have different risks to the shoulder. The alternative spiking method is said to be a possible prevention to some injuries that occur in the shoulder and also enhance an athletes performance.

Jumper's knee

Jumper's knee is injury term used in volleyball circles that describes the mechanism of the injury known as patella tendinopathy, patella tendinosis or patella tendonitis. Jumper's knee is defined as a syndrome of tendon pain, localized tenderness and that is detrimental to an athletes performance. in the initial phase of the Jumper's knee injury the tendons with the knee are usually inflamed. If Jumper's knee becomes a chronic injury ,which usually occurs as age increases, the tendons show an increasing degree of degeneration and little to no inflation present. As the etiology and pathology of Jumper's knee is not known the treatment varies and is largely based on a trial and error basis.

Jumpers knee is said to occur after frequent actions involving quick accelerations and declarations, eccentric activities and quick cutting actions.As spiking involves jumping, in which a quick acceleration occurs when jumping and quick deceleration when landing, this action is a possible cause of Jumper's knee. Also blocking is a possible cause of Jumper's knee because it to involves jumping and landing quickly. However, Jumper's knee is less common among athletes who compete in beach volleyball rather than those who play indoor volleyball. This is because beach volleyball is played on sand which reduces the impact of landing on the knee.

Preventative Measures, Treatment, and Other Common Injuries

There are ways to prevent injuries such as stretching, proper hydration, conditioning, and more. Also, knee pads are necessary to help avoid knee injuries and ankle braces are often used as a way to stabilize the ankles when jumping. The most common volleyball associated injuries are found in the ankles, fingers, shoulders, knees, and the back.

These include rotator cuff tendentious, ACL tear, patellar tendonitis, ligament tears or dislocation in fingers, ankle sprains, and low back pain associated with stress or a herniated disk. Treatment for these injuries includes physical therapy, strength training, and occasionally surgery or a brace. If surgery is needed, the time to return to play may vary depending on the severity of the injury. For a torn ACL, recovery to return is anywhere from 6 to 9 months. Often volleyball injuries are due to poor form when blocking and receiving a serve or a hit. Certainly, there are times where the injuries cannot be prevented and are simply accidental. To avoid injuries, conditioning and stretching are very important as well as correctly executing each play.

5

Basic Rules & Regulations for Playing Volleyball

In volleyball, players work together to return the ball over the net in three hits or fewer, without letting the ball touch the ground. The USA Volleyball and International Federation of Volleyball rule books provide the standard rules for competitive men's and women's volleyball in the United States.

Court

The standard competitive volleyball court measures 59 feet long by 29.6 feet wide. The center line runs under the net, dividing the court into two equal sides. An attack line runs 9 feet, 10 inches behind the net on each side of the court. The attack line divides the front and back zones. The net measures 8 feet, 11 5/8 inches tall for standard men's competition and 7 feet, 4 1/8 inches tall for standard women's competition, according to the USA Volleyball and International Federation of Volleyball rule books.

Players

Both teams must have six players on the court to begin play. Players follow the proper rotational order through each set. Players rotate between six positions on the court, including three back-row positions behind the attack line and three front-row positions in front of the attack line. Each time a team gains the right to serve, its players must rotate one position clockwise. Once the server contacts the ball, players can move out of their rotational positions to play the point. Players in a back-row position must not attack the ball above the net and in front of the attack line, however.

Serve

Team captains complete a coin toss before the game to determine the team that will serve first. The player in the back right position in the rotation serves the ball. To serve, players must stand behind the court's end line and hit the ball out of the air. If the serve hits the net or lands out of bounds, the server's team loses the point. The same player continues to serve until his team loses a point. When a team loses a point on its serve, the other team gains the right to serve.

Play

Teams must return the ball over the net in three hits or fewer. Blocks do not count toward the team's hit total. If one player hits the ball twice in succession or contacts the ball illegally by palming, catching or throwing it, her team loses the point. If a back-row player attacks the ball illegally, his team loses the point. If any player touches the net or net posts, her team loses the point. Teams win points when the opposing team commits a violation, fails to return the ball over the net, lets the ball touch the ground inbounds or hits the ball into the net or out of bounds.

Scoring

Teams can win points on their own serve and on their opponent's serve, according to the USA Volleyball and International Federation of Volleyball rule books. The first team to win 25 points with a two-point lead wins the set. The first team to win three sets wins the match. If the match goes to a fifth set, the first team to win 15 points with a two-point lead wins the set and the match.

GENERAL VOLLEYBALLGAMEPLAY

A point or rally is started when one team serves the ball. The player serving the ball must stand behind the end line or restraining line at the back of the court until after they have contacted the volleyball. To serve a player hits the ball with their hand over the net and into the opposing team's side. If the ball doesn't go over the net or hits the ground, the point is over. The opposing team must now return the ball without letting it hit the ground.

They can hit the ball up to three times. No single player can hit the ball twice in a row (blocks don't count). Typically a team will try to set up an attack. They use the first two hits to set the ball for a spike or hard hit over the net. The two teams continue hitting the ball back and forth until the point ends. A point can end by one team hitting a winning shot that hits the ground within the opponent's court or by one team causing a fault and losing the point.

Which volleyball team serves the ball is determined by the previous point. Whoever won the previous point, gets to serve next. At the start of a match, the first serve is determined by a volley.

Team Rotation

Although players play certain roles on a volleyball team, they all must play all positions. There are three players on the front line and three in the back. Each time a team gains the serve they must rotate. The entire team rotates in a clockwise manner with one player moving to the front line and another player moving to the back line. This way each player plays each spot.

Scoring

Scoring in volleyball is pretty simple, but it also has changed over time. Most matches are divided up into sets. A typical match may be a best of 5 sets where the first team to win 5 sets wins the match. In each set, the first team to 25 points wins as long as they are 2 points ahead. A point is scored on every rally, regardless of which team serves.

It used to be that only the volleyball team serving could score a point on a won rally. Also, sets were typically played to 15 points. This was changed in 1999.

Volleyball Faults

There are several ways to fault and lose the point. Here are some examples:

- Hitting the volleyball illegally - you must strike the ball in a manner such that you don't hold the ball or palm, carry, or throw it.
- Stepping over or on the line while serving
- Not hitting the ball over the net
- Touching the net
- Reaching under the net and interfering with a player or the ball
- Not serving in the correct order
- Hitting the volleyball out of bounds
- Double hitting - when the same player hits the ball twice in a row
- Hitting the ball more than 3 times

NFHS RULES GOVERN PLAY WITH THE FOLLOWING MODIFICATIONS

The Game

Players may play on one team in each league. A team competes with 6 players, however, minimum number of players is 3. All players must be registered and checked in before the game begins.

Rock/paper/scissors determines which team receives the choice of either the serve or the court.

The best of three games will win matches. Each non-deciding game will be won by the team that first scores 25 points with a minimum two-point advantage (no scoring cap). If there is a deciding game, it will be won by the team that first scores 15 points with a minimum two-point advantage (no scoring cap). Point will be scored on each rally. If the receiving team wins the rally, they score a point and gain the serve.

Rest periods between games of a match shall be no longer than 2 minutes.

Each team is permitted 2, 30-second team time-outs per game. Time-outs may be requested to an official only when the ball is dead and are not in effect until the official recognizes the time-out with a whistle or hand signal and vocal command.

Players are asked to wear tennis shoes for their own protection. We will not permit anyone to play with hard-soled shoes or sandals. Participants with casts (especially hand or wrist) will not be allowed to participate. Leave all jewelry at home. The IM Department strongly recommends that no jewelry be worn in IM competition. Do not chase loose volleyballs into other courts while play is in progress.

The Serve

The server has 5 seconds to begin the serve from the time the official signals the serve with a whistle.

The service zone includes the full width of the 9-meter area behind the end lines. The server may move freely within the service zone. At the moment of the service hit or takeoff for a jump service, the server must be completely in the service zone and not touching the court (end line included) or the playing service outside the zone. After the service, the player may skip or land outside the zone including the court.

If the server tosses the ball and does not serve it he does NOT need to let it bounce before he re-tosses it.

Net Service Is In Play. A served ball that hits the net does not result in the service team losing its serve. The net serve is considered in-play, unless 1) it does not continue over the net or 2) lands outside the opposing team's court-side untouched by the opposing team.

Spiking & Blocking

The receiving team is not allowed to block or spike a served ball.

A spiker must contact the ball on his/her own side of the net, but may in the course of the follow through reach over (but not touch) the net.

Back line players while inside the attack zone (10 feet from the net) may not play the ball directly into the opposite court if contact is made when any part of the ball is above the top of the net.

The team that has affected the block shall have the right to three more contacts, with the blocker having the right to make the first of the three allowable hits.

Net Play

A ball hit into the net, may still be kept in play (up to 3 hits) provided that a player does not make contact with the net.

Players may not touch the net. If 2 opposing players touch the net simultaneously, the ball is declared dead and is replayed.

Ground Rules

A ball is out of bounds and becomes dead when it:

1. Touches any part of a backboard or its supports hanging in a vertical position
2. The IM West or IM East vertical glass backboards and supporting structures are considered out of bounds.
3. Makes contact with the side walls (including the slanted walls of the running track at IM East).

A ball hitting the ceiling or an overhead obstruction (lights, fan, or basketball hoop lying horizontally) above a playable area shall remain in play provided the ball contacts the ceiling or obstruction on the side of the net that is occupied by the team that last played the ball.

Legal Play

The ball must be returned over the net in 3 hits or less.

It is legal to contact the ball with any part of the body as long as the ball rebounds immediately. It may not "lay" against the body or forcefully kicked. If a player touches the ball or the ball touches a player, it is considered as a play on the ball. Except in the following case: A ball touching the body more than once in succession is legal when played off a hard-driven spiked ball, or blocked and played again by the blocker.

If 2 players on the same team contact the ball simultaneously, it counts as one contact, and any player may play the ball.

One may play the ball twice during a volley, but not twice in succession, unless played directly off a block.

When a ball touches a boundary line, it is considered in play.

Rule of Three (3): If a ball is played by more than two players on a team, the ball must be played by both genders. The order is not relevant. If three contacts of the same gender occur the official will blow the play dead and award the opposing team the serve and the point.

Illegal Play

Players are not permitted to scoop, hold, and lift or push the ball. The ball may never be contacted with an open-hand underhanded motion.

In addition, during the first hit of the team, except when serving, the ball may contact various parts of the body consecutively, provided the contacts occur during one action.

An official may (at their own discretion) penalize a team one point or loss of serve for intentionally delaying the game.

Substitutions

Each team may choose to rotate extra players into the server's position on a continuous basis. In all substitutions participants must inform the official on the net and wait for the official to initiate the substitution.

All substitutions must be made within a 15-second time limit. If changing time exceeds 15 seconds, a team time-out will be charged. If a team has none of its 2 allotted team time-outs remaining, point or side-out will be awarded to the other team. An injury substitution is not considered as one of the 2 allowable time outs.

If a player arrives after the first game of the match has started, and her/his name is on the roster, that player will be allowed to play in the game as a substitute if the team uses regular substitutions.

Conduct

Unsporting conduct includes actions which are unbecoming to an ethical, fair, and honorable individual. it consists of acts of deceit, disrespect or vulgarity, and includes taunting.

No player, teammate, coach and/or team attendant shall act in an unsporting manner while on or near the court before, during, or after a contest.

Unsporting conduct includes, but is not limited to: disconcertion, attempting to influence the decision of a referee, disrespectfully adressing a referee, questioning a referee's judgment, showing disgust with referees' decisions, disrespectfully addressing, baiting, or taunting anyone invlolved in the contest, making any excessive requests designed to disrupt the contest, and using profane/vulgar language.

Unsporting conduct shall be penalized as follows: 1) a verbal warning from a referee for the first minor offense 2) yellow card for a second minor offense 3) red card for first serious offense or third minor offense. The accumulation of two yellow cards or one red card will result in player ejection. Any player ejected for unsportsmanlike conduct will be required to leave the facility (out of sight, out of sound) and will be required to serve a suspension from Intramural competition.

Any player who accumulates three yellow cards throughout the season will be required to serve a suspension.

Any team who accumulates three yellow cards, two yellow cards and one red card, or two red cards during a contest will forfeit that contest.

Forfeits

GAME TIME IS FORFEIT TIME! Teams are strongly encouraged to arrive 15 minutes early for their games. Any game whose outcome is declared a forfeit will result in a loss being credited to the forfeiting team. A forfeit will be declared under the following conditions:

1. A team does not field the required number of eligible players by the designated game time.
2. A violation of any rule as stated in the Intramural Sports Code of Conduct.

In the event of a multiple forfeits by the same team, that team will not be eligible for playoff competition.

Multiple forfeits may also result in the team being dropped from the league prior to the completion of the regular season; teams that are removed due to forfeits are not eligible to receive refunds.

Note

It is University policy that alcoholic beverages may not be consumed in University recreational areas.

Please cooperate with the Intramural Department in keeping both your players and spectators from bringing alcohol to the building. Any person or teams that consume alcoholic beverages before a game will not be permitted to participate. Opponents, officials and supervisors are responsible to report such incidents.

Co-rec Modifications

A team consists of 6 players, 3 women/ 3 men or 4 women/ 2 men. Teams may compete with 3, 4, or 5 players in the following male/female ratios: 2 women/ 1 man, 1 woman/ 2 men, 2 women/ 2 men, 3 women/ 2 men, 2 women/ 3 men.

The serving order must alternate men and women. (Exception, 2/1 and 3/2 player ratio)

The net height will be co-rec height (7'8").

VOLLEYBALL ROTATION RULES

In volleyball, there are six players on the court for each team. Each player starts in a specific location, but these locations are not to be confused with player positions-(setter, middle blocker, outside hitter, opposite or libero). Each player, with the exception of the libero, will rotate to each location in a clockwise manner before each serve.

Front row players stand nearer to the net and are responsible for blocking or hitting, while back row players are positioned in the middle or back of the court and are responsible for digging or defence. Back row players (with the exception of the libero) can attack the ball as long as they jump for the attack before the attack line.

Each time a team wins a point or before they start the serve, the serving team rotates clockwise.

If players move out of their locations before the ball is served, they will be called for overlapping or being out of position. A point is then awarded to the other team. If the team at fault was serving, the ball will be passed to the opposing team for service. Players need to be mindful of their locations and make sure they are in the right place in relation to their teammates.

Player positions are judged by the placement of their feet. Each front row player must have one foot on the court closer to the net than the feet of the player directly behind them. Players will rotate locations each time their team makes a serve, with the player in the RB location typically the server. If the serving team wins the point, the player who served the ball will do so till they lose a point.

NEWTON'S THREE LAWS OF MOTION FOR VOLLEYBALL

Here's a fun thought: Next time you watch the fast-paced action of a volleyball game, consider how many laws of physics are being demonstrated on the court. For example, every movement by the ball or the athletes illustrates one of Newton's three laws of motion: inertia, acceleration and action-reaction. Applying the principles of physics to sports does more than just provide an interesting math problem. These analyses form the basis of biomechanics and sports science and can be used to improve athletic performance.

Three Laws Plus One Force

Newton's first law, also known as the law of inertia, states that unless acted upon by a force, a motionless body will stay still or a moving body will keep moving. The law of acceleration, Newton's second law, states that an increase in the velocity of a moving object is directly proportional to the force applied and inversely proportional to the object's mass. The third law, the law of action and reaction, states when one object exerts a force on another object, the latter object reacts with an equal force in the opposite direction.

A critical component involved in these laws of motion is called force, which pulls or pushes on an object and creates movement. Force isn't directly visible but is measured by the direction and distance a moving object travels.

Inertia: Get a Move On

A nice example of the law of inertia can be seen in a volleyball at the highest arc of a server's toss, that moment when the ball is nearly motionless. It will either fall straight down due to the force of gravity, or sail across the net from the force of a hand striking it. In an example of a moving object, a spiked volleyball moves in a fairly straight line downwards unless deflected by the force of the net, receiver's forearms, blocker's hands or floor.

Acceleration: Lighter is Quicker

The law of acceleration comes into play every time a volleyball player moves on the court. Smaller athletes are more agile on the court because their lower mass accelerates and decelerates more quickly, which is particularly critical on defense. Heavier athletes need more time to get into position, or more leg strength to get there as quickly. The faster the arm swing, the more force is exerted on a spiked volleyball at the moment of contact.

Action-Reaction: Use the Force

The law of opposing forces can be seen when volleyball players leap off the floor. The force exerted by their feet downwards is countered by an opposing, upwards force exerted by the floor. If the floor didn't "push back," athletes wouldn't be able to leave the ground. The opposing force from the floor, by the way, is also why people get sore feet after a long practice session and bruised from hitting the floor after a hard dig.

NEWTON AND VOLLEYBALL

Part 1 (Inertia): An object at rest will remain at rest unless acted upon by an unbalanced force.

In volleyball: The ball will not go anywhere until someone serves it.

Part 2: (momentum): An object in motion will remain in motion in a straight line at a constant speed unless acted upon by an unbalanced force.

In volleyball: Once served the ball will travel in an arc due to earth's gravity but will go in one direction only unless someone hits it to change its direction or speed. Then it will continue in the new direction and speed until someone else hits it.

Newton's Second Law:

Force equals mass times acceleration: $f = m \times a$

In volleyball: The harder you hit the ball the faster it will go it whatever direction you hit it. Also, the ball won't go over the net unless you hit it hard enough. Also, if you hit the ball too hard it will go out of bounds. Also, a lighter ball will go farther and faster than a heavier ball.

Newton's Third Law:

For every action there is an equal and opposite reaction.

In volleyball: The ball hits your hand just as hard as you hit the ball. To avoid injuring your fingers, hold your hand in the proper position. Also, to make the ball go where you want it to go your must hit it in the proper spot with the proper force.

VOLLEYBALL RULES AND REGULATIONS

Volleyball is a team sport where two teams, typically with six players on each team, are separated by a net. The players on the two teams hit an inflated ball back and forth over the net, trying to avoid having the ball hit the ground on their side of the net. To put it in simple terms, volleyball is a team sport in which the goal is to keep the ball alive while it is on your side of the net but to kill the rally by putting the ball down on your opponent's side of the net.

Volleyball is an exciting, fast-paced sport. It has been an official part of the Summer Olympic Games since 1964.

Rules

The complete set of rules for volleyball is extremely extensive. Additionally, volleyball rules can be difficult to keep up with as they often change. However, many of the central, most critical rules of the sport remain the same.

You can score points in the game of volleyball in one of two ways:

Putting the ball on the floor in-bounds on your opponent's side of the net.

An error (forced or unforced) by your opponent which renders them unable to return the ball over the net and in-bounds on your side in their allotted three contacts.

The sport of volleyball is one of the most malleable sports because it is played in many variations and on many different surfaces.

Teams

Volleyball can be played in teams, with anywhere between two and six players. Indoor volleyball is usually played with six players on each team.

Beach volleyball is often played with two players. Four-person volleyball is often seen in grass tournaments and also occasionally on the beach.

Variations

There are many variations to the game of volleyball. Where volleyball is played, along with how it is scored can vary widely. Volleyball can be played on hardwood, grass, sand or asphalt, using rally or side-out scoring.

Volleyball matches can be played as one game or as the best of three or best of five sets. As far as scoring, volleyball can be played to 15, 25, 30 or any number of points technically.

Play begins with one team serving the ball to the other. Each time the ball crosses over the net, a team gets three contacts before they must send the ball back to the opponent's side. Ideally, the three contacts will be a pass, set and hit, but it can be three passes or any other combination of contacts as long as they are legal contacts.

The rally (or volley) continues until the ball hits the ground or one of the rules is broken. The team that is not responsible for the end of the rally then gets a point.

A Few Volleyball No-No's

You cannot:

- Touch the net while making a play on the ball
- Step on the back line while serving (foot fault)
- Contact the ball more than three times on a side (A block doesn't count as a contact)
- Lift or push the ball
- Play the ball over the net outside of the antennas
- Contact the ball twice in a row (unless the first contact was a block.)

Winning the Match

The first team to score the agreed upon number of points wins the game. You must win by at least two points. The teams switch sides, the next game starts with a score of 0-0 and play starts again.

In a best-of-five match, the team who wins three sets wins the match.

6

Volleyball Officials and Their Duties

Professional officiating ensures any game is played fairly and according to the rules. In volleyball, officials also ensure points are earned properly and awarded when deserved. Those given the title of official during a volleyball game include the referees, the scorekeeper, assistant scorekeeper, or libero tracker, and the line judges.

As in most sporting competitions, volleyball employs referees in order to control the flow of the game and enforce the rules. The volleyball referee team includes the first referee, the second referee, the scorer and two line judges. Without the referee team, the fast-paced game could easily get out of hand if disputes regarding rules were to arise.

REFEREES

Find the referee at the center of the court, dressed in black and white stripes. A referee's duties include signaling when a rally begins and ends. The referee is also responsible for officially recognizing team requests, substitutions, time-outs and communicating with the coaches at the appropriate times. Multiple referees may oversee a match.

SCOREKEEPER

Before play begins, the scorekeeper records team and player information. Once the game begins, scorekeepers not only track points, but also player substitutions, sanctions and time-outs. The scorekeeper keeps an eye on the individual serving the ball to track the rotation and notify referees of potential lapses. At the close of the game, the scorekeeper records the final score of the game.

Assistant Scorekeeper

The assistant scorekeeper or libero tracker is responsible for updating the scoreboard and keeping an eye on the libero. The libero tracking duty was added in 1999. This individual records changes in the libero rotation, notifying referees when problems occur in the rotation.

Scorers

The official scorer keeps track of the score throughout the volleyball game. Before the game begins the scorer notes the starting lineup of each team and notifies the referees if the lineup wasn't received on time.

If a dispute or irregularity arises regarding the score, the scorer uses a buzzer to notify the first and second referees. Additionally, when a substitution request arises, the scorer notifies the referees.

Line Judges

There are usually two line judges, one at either end of the court and in opposite corners. Line judges work with the referees, signaling to assist in making judgment calls. These officials often use flags to signal when a ball is in or out, hits the antennae of the net, or when the server commits a foot fault, or steps outside the line, as they serve.

At least two, and as many as four, line judges monitor each game. The line judges stand at the corners of the court watching the lines to indicate whether a ball in play falls in or out of the court.

If a server steps on the line during a serve, the line judge watching the given line notifies the referees using a flag. When a player touches an out-of-play ball or if the ball hits an antenna, the designated line judge also indicates the interference.

First Referee

The first referee stands on the referee stand and controls the play of the entire game. Whatever issues arise during the game, the first referee determines the call and the has the final say. After making a call, no player or other referee can argue the call, although a formal protest can be placed with the scorer.

Before the match begins, the first referee inspects the equipment and the players' uniforms. The warm-ups and the coin toss also fall under the jurisdiction of the first referee.

Throughout the match, the first referee makes calls regarding faults and scoring issues. Following the match, the first referee notes the score and signs the official paperwork.

Second Referee

The second referee works to assist the first referee throughout the game. If for some reason the first referee can't finish her duties, the second referee may take the place of the first referee.

The second referee stands next to the post opposite the first referee. In addition to assisting the first referee with determining faults throughout the game, the second referee is in charge of all substitutions, timeouts and the actions of the scorer.

Timer and Umpire

The umpire assists the referee in his duties throughout the game, particularly when it comes to play around the net and center line. He stands opposite the referee, outside the sideline boundary and back from the standard. The timer sits with the scorer and ensures the clock is working properly. He takes direction from the referees as to when to start and stop play. The timer times pre-match warmups as well as the three-minute intermissions between games. The timer is also expected to give an audio signal when the improper player has served or another rule infraction occurs.

PROCEDURES FOR FIRST AND SECOND OFFICIALS

Of the two volleyball referees, the first referee is known as the up official or head referee. In USA or FIVB competition, the first referee is usually referred to as the first official or R1.

In high school volleyball, the down referee is also known as theumpire.

In USA or FIVB competition, the second referee is usually referred to as the second official or R2.

USAV rules somewhat differ from High School and other volleyball competitions. With this fact, it's important to become familiar with the different rules for playing.

As a player, coach, or referee, you should be familiar with the rules to get that competitive edge.

First Official (R1 or up referee) –- Volleyball Referees

The first referee is the official that stands on the referee stand (raised platform) positioned at on the side of the court across from the team benches. It is the first referee that starts play by whistling and signaling (beckoning) the server to serve the ball.

The first referee is the official in charge. If they feel it's necessary to do so, the first referee has the authority to overrule any of the other officials (second referee scorekeeper, libero tracker, or line judges).

Also, the first referee may have officials replaced if it is needed.

The volleyball referees should discuss before the match on what the second referee needs to signal to the first referee (illegal ball handling, illegal back row and blocks and attacks, etc.).

THE FIRST REFEREE...

Whistle any violations It is the first referees responsibility to whistle any and all violations they see. If possible, the second referee should whistle net violations, centerline violations, serve receive position faults, and serving order violations. If the second official doesn't catch these violations, the first referee has the authority to make the call.

Whistle player mishandling the ball Only the first referee has the authority to whistle ball handling (lifts, double contacts, 4 hits, etc.). If appropriate, the second referee may discretely signal ball handling to the first referee.

Giving Sanctions Only the first referee has the authority to issue sanctions to players, coaches, etc.

First Referee Pre-match Duties include...

- Inspects equipment/identifies ground rules
- Directs informative Captain's meeting
- Briefs officiating team
- Observes setters during Warm-Up

Mechanics...

- Scans court prior to each beckon
- Is approachable but assertive
- Communicates effectively with captains/coaches

- Gives scorekeeper enough time to record subs

Judgment...

- Call prolonged contact power dinks
- Call prolonged contact 2nd or 3rd hit
- Calls lifts out of net correctly (not automatically)
- Judges setter/non-setter ball handling the same
- Recognizes and calls back row violations
- Recognizes and calls overlaps and screens
- Is preventative whenever possible
- Assesses penalties appropriately

Poise...

- Confident and alert appearance
- Is aware of entire court/playing area
- Has good reaction time on calls
- Directs/Controls when necessary

Critical Elements...

- Has whistle, cards and coin
- Whistle is clear, sharp and authoritative
- Signals are correct, visible, held
- Whistles ball dead immediately, then signals
- Ability to stay with the play
- Uses R2 & lines people effectively
- Good eye contact with R2
- Calls 1st hit, prolonged contact vs multiple contact
- Calls multiple contacts on 2nd & 3rd hit
- Consistent judgment calls.

Second Official (R2 or down referee) – Volleyball Referees

The second referee is concerned with matters such as keeping time, assisting the first referee in making calls,administering substitutions, and verbally communicating with team coaches. The second referee also needs to communicate effectively with the scorekeeper.

The second referee should overlook the scorekeeper with recording subs, timeouts, etc. The second referee should help the scorekeeper and libero tracker with any questions or issues that come up.

The second referee (or umpire) stands on the ground on the opposite side of the court from the first referee. The second referee should position themselves so they can effectively transition from one side of the net to the other when the ball is in play.

The second referees main responsibility is to manage the court, that is, communicate effectively with players and coaches at the team bench area, the work crew at the scores table, the line judges, and first referee.

The second referee should assist the first referee (hand signaling the first referee or blowing the whistle to make calls) in order for the match to run as smoothly as possible.

THE SECOND REFEREE...

Watch teams for overlaps during the serve Watch the receiving team at the moment the ball is served for overlaps.

Switching sides of the net The second referee switches positions one side of the net to the other during the match, always staying on the side opposite the ball.

Handles substitutions The second referee administers subs, making sure the subs are recorded properly on the scoresheet. When the scorekeeper has finished recording the subs, a hand signal is given to the first referee signaling play is ready.

Handles time outs When a coach or team captain calls time out, the second referee should blow the whistle and signal time out. The second referee times the time outs, whistles at the end of time, and signals how many time outs have been taken by each team.

Volleyball Officials Second Referee

The second referee is the down referee. Also referred to as the R2.

The R2 has specific duties.

Pre-match Duties...

- Ensures game ball is ready
- Attends Captain's meeting
- Informs Scorekeeper of coin flip result
- Times Warm-Up
- Collects line-up sheets on time
- Verifies line-ups/player position on courts
- Identifies captains to R1

Mechanics...

- Whistles/signals to begin & end time-out
- Whistles/signals substitutions
- Whistles/signal to end time between games

Teamwork...

- Communicates effectively with scorekeeper
- Assists R1; Discreet signals (4 hits, etc.)
- Is approachable but assertive

Judgment...

- Recognizes and calls overlaps
- Whistles ball outside or over antenna (R2 side)
- Whistles ball outside playing area behind R1
- Calls/Assists with back row violations

Bench Management...

- Pays attention/communicates with bench/coach
- Anticipates, recognizes, controls subs/time-outs
- Manages time-outs (subs off court, spills, etc)

Critical Elements

- Has whistle, watch and coin
- Whistle is clear, sharp and authoritative
- Signals are correct, visible, holds/steps out
- Mimics R1, signals (not service beckon)
- Calls net fouls and centerline violations
- Stands away from net pole/standard
- Good eye contact with R1
- Check receiving team on each service
- Focuses on defensive team side
- Transitions (side to side) quickly

VOLLEYBALL REFEREE RULES & HAND SIGNALS

Volleyball is a competitive game played by men and women. Children as young as 7 years old can begin playing this sport as well as adults. League volleyball has increased in popularity since the 1990s and college volleyball is watched by many. You should be aware of a number of rules and hand signals performed by the referees if you play the game.

Referees

Referees are the officials who are responsible for ensuring that all rules of the games are followed. Two official referees are in any volleyball game. The first referee, or R1, stands at the referee stand. The first official gives the signal to start the game by whistling and has the authority to overrule any other official's decision. The second referee, or R2, is responsible for keeping track of time, administrating the substitutes and communicating with the coaches or teams effectively as well as assisting the first official.

Hand Signals

Referees use several hand signals during a volleyball game. The referee blows the whistle to signal the start and end of each play. The hand signals are given by the referee who first signals the fault and then indicates which team has won the point. A point is indicated by one finger at the side of the court to indicate the winner of the rally. Ball in bounds is meant to show the point of the court where the ball landed and is indicated by pointing one arm and hand toward the floor. If a ball is out of bounds or went outside the antenna, the referee will raise his forearms vertically and palm facing inwards. A carry is when the ball had too much contact time with the players hand and is indicated by holding hand horizontal with the palm facing upwards. A double hit is indicated by two fingers showing that the player contacted the ball twice. Begin service is meant to indicate that the server is now allowed to serve, which can be shown by holding the hand high in the air with the palm in the direction of the team serving the ball. A net violation is meant to show that there was a contact with the net. This can be shown by placing a hand over the net, ensuring that the palm is facing down.

Volleyball Terms

Player, coaches and referees should know certain volleyball terms. These basic volleyball terms include an ace, which is a serve that makes a direct point and a kill occurs when an attack results in immediate point. A tip is placing a soft shot above the opponents block, a block occurs when the player blocks a spiked ball resulting in the ball returning to the spiker's court and a free ball is a ball that is returned by passing. A set means placing the ball near the net for spiking purpose. Other terms include a spike, which is powering the ball over the net by hitting it hard, a dig is returning the spiked ball and a tool is spiking the ball off the opponent's block.

Violations

Violations may occur in which the referee will need to call. Violations include a serving violation, which indicates the ball was not served within eight seconds of blowing the whistle, a net violation means that the net was touched, an attack violation is related to hitting the ball from an illegal position and a blocking violation is related to blocking the ball even before it has crossed the net into the player's own court.

THE AUTHORITY OF THE REFEREE

Each match is controlled by a referee who has full authority to enforce the Laws of the Game in connection with the match.

Decisions of the referee

Decisions will be made to the best of the referee's ability according to the Laws of the Game and the spirit of the game and will be based on the opinion of the referee who has the discretion to take appropriate action within the framework of the Laws of the Game.

The decisions of the referee regarding facts connected with play, including whether or not a goal is scored and the result of the match, are final. The decisions of the referee, and all other match officials, must always be respected.

The referee may only change a decision on realising that it is incorrect or on the advice of another match official, provided play has not restarted or the referee has signalled the end of the first or second half (including extra time) and left the field of play or terminated the match.

If a referee is incapacitated, play may continue under the supervision of the other match officials until the ball is next out of play.

Powers and duties

The referee:

- enforces the Laws of the Game
- controls the match in cooperation with the other match officials
- acts as timekeeper, keeps a record of the match and provides the appropriate authorities with a match report, including information on disciplinary action and any other incidents that occurred before, during or after the match
- supervises and/or indicates the restart of play

Advantage

- allows play to continue when an offence occurs and the non-offending team will benefit from the advantage and penalises the offence if the anticipated advantage does not ensue at that time or within a few seconds

Disciplinary Action

- punishes the more serious offence, in terms of sanction, restart, physical severity and tactical impact, when more than one offence occurs at the same time
- takes disciplinary action against players guilty of cautionable and sending-off offences
- has the authority to take disciplinary action from entering the field of play for the pre-match inspection until leaving the field of play after the match ends (including kicks from the penalty mark). If, before entering the field of play at the start of the match, a player commits a sending-off offence, the referee has the authority to prevent the player taking

part in the match; the referee will report any other misconduct

- has the power to show yellow or red cards and, where competition rules permit, temporarily dismiss a player, from entering the field of play at the start of the match until after the match has ended, including during the half-time interval, extra time and kicks from the penalty mark

- takes action against team officials who fail to act in a responsible manner and may expel them from the field of play and its immediate surrounds; a medical team official who commits a dismissible offence may remain if the team has no other medical person available, and act if a player needs medical attention

- acts on the advice of other match officials regarding incidents that the referee has not seen

Injuries

- allows play to continue until the ball is out of play if a player is only slightly injured

- stops play if a player is seriously injured and ensures that the player is removed from the field of play. An injured player may not be treated on the field of play and may only re-enter after play has restarted; if the ball is in play, re-entry must be from the touchline but if the ball is out of play, it may be from any boundary line. Exceptions to the requirement to leave the field of play are only when:

- a goalkeeper is injured

- a goalkeeper and an outfield player have collided and need attention

- players from the same team have collided and need attention

- a severe injury has occurred

- a player is injured as the result of a physical offence for which the opponent is cautioned or sent off (e.g. reckless or serious foul challenge), if the assessment/treatment is completed quickly

- ensures that any player bleeding leaves the field of play. The player may only re-enter on receiving a signal from the referee, who must be satisfied that the bleeding has stopped and there is no blood on the equipment

- if the referee has authorised the doctors and /or stretcher bearers to enter the field of play, the player must leave on a stretcher or on foot. A player who does not comply, must be cautioned for unsporting behaviour

- if the referee has decided to caution or send off a player who is injured and has to leave the field of play for treatment, the card must be shown before the player leaves

- if play has not been stopped for another reason, or if an injury suffered by a player is not the result of an offence, play is restarted with a dropped ball

Outside Interference

- stops, suspends or abandons the match for any offences or because of outside interference e.g. if:

- the floodlights are inadequate

- an object thrown by a spectator hits a match official, a player or team official, the referee may allow the match to continue, or stop, suspend or abandon it depending on the severity of the incident

- a spectator blows a whistle which interferes with play - play is stopped and restarted with a dropped ball

- an extra ball, other object or animal enters the field of play during the match, the referee must:

- stop play (and restart with a dropped ball) only if it interferes with play unless the ball is going into the goal and the interference does not prevent a defending player playing the ball, the goal is awarded if the ball enters the goal (even if contact was made with the ball) unless the ball enters the opponents' goal

- allow play to continue if it does not interfere with play and have it removed at the earliest possible opportunity
- allows no unauthorised persons to enter the field of play

Referee's Equipment

Compulsory Equipment

- Whistle(s)
- Watch(es)
- Red and yellow cards
- Notebook (or other means of keeping a record of the match)

Other Equipment

Referees may be permitted to use:

- Equipment for communicating with other match officials – buzzer/bleep flags, headsets etc….
- EPTS or other fitness monitoring equipment

Referees and other match officials are prohibited from wearing jewellery or electronic equipment

Referee signals

Refer to graphics for approved referee signals.

In addition to the current 'two armed' signal for an advantage, a similar 'one arm' signal is now permitted as it is not always easy for referees to run with both arms extended.

VOLLEYBALL REFEREE RULES & HAND SIGNALS

Four officials oversee a volleyball game, in addition to an official scorekeeper. The main referee takes an elevated position along the net opposite the teams' benches and the score table. A second referee is positioned on the floor at the net, directly in front of the score table. Two line officials take positions at corners of the court, diagonal from each other, to assist in making calls regarding the landing of the ball inside or outside the lines. The officials control the game by enforcing the rules and use hand signals to indicate most of the calls they make.

Boundary Lines

Volleyball officials monitor the boundary lines on the court, calling balls in or out depending on where they strike the court. The line officials are usually the first to make the call, but the main referee at the net is able to overrule line calls. Two hands extended forward at about waist height with the palms facing down toward the court indicate that a ball is inside the line. Two arms extended straight up over the head with the palms of the hands facing backward indicate that the ball is out.

Point

The main referee indicates when a point is concluded and to whom the point is awarded. After blowing her whistle, she will point with one hand at the court on the side of the net where the ball hit the floor. This signals the end of that point. She then extends her arm and points to the service line of the team that won that point—using her arm that corresponds to that side of the court—indicating that it has earned control of the serve for the next point.

Player in the Net

Volleyball players must not break the plane of the net by either making contact with the net or stepping beyond the center line on the court. When a player violates this rule, the point is awarded to the other team. The referee will tap the net with an open hand on the side of the net on which the violation occurred to acknowledge the call.

Serve

The player serving the ball cannot initiate play until instructed to do so by the main net referee. The official signals the player to serve by extending his arm in the direction of the server with is palm facing up. After blowing the whistle, he then moves his hand in a sweeping direction over his head toward the other side of the net.

Game

Volleyball matches are broken into games. The usual match is played in a best-three-of-five format in which the match ends when one team wins three games. The first four games of a match are played to 25 points. When one team reaches 25, it must be leading by at least two points to capture the game. Once that occurs, the main official indicates that the game is over by crossing her arms across her chest. She then indicates that the two teams switch ends of the court for the next game by passing one arm across the front of her body at waist height, and the other arm across her back at waist height. If a best-of-five match goes to a fifth game, the teams do not switch ends for the fifth game, and that game is played to 15 points instead of 25.

PRE-MATCH SAFETY RESPONSIBILITIES FOR VOLLEYBALL OFFICIALS

Taking care of pre-match responsibilities is an important stepping-stone in preparing officials to officiate the match. Once the officials arrive at the site of the match there are important procedures and guidelines that must be followed to ensure the safety of the participants, officials, and spectators.

Throughout my 27 years of officiating I have entered many sites that have equipment stored in what would be playable areas for the participants. Wrestling mats, rebounding machines, physical education equipment, and other objects are often encountered when officials arrive at the site. Many times officials are told that there is no other place to store this equipment. It is the responsibility of the officials to ask the administration of the school to take care of this problem and explain why it must be removed in a professional manner. Different states have procedures for officials to address this problem such as special reports to their state association, local official's boards meeting with athletic directors and principals, written correspondence between officials, coaches, and administrators, to name a few. The most important aspect in taking care of safety issues is for local officiating boards to discuss safety in their meetings, carefully discussing potential and specific safety dynamics at each school where they will be officiating. Once issues have been identified pro-active steps must be taken to eliminate all safety issues at each site. This is extremely beneficial for new officials and a reminder for veteran officials.

A good way to identify safety problems is for the local boards to ensure that there is a visit to each site where they will be officiating before the season begins. This is helpful in many ways. It gives officials and coaches the opportunity to meet each other and to discuss safety problem areas at the site. Often coaches can take care of the issues themselves or ask their administrators to assist in solving the problem areas before the season begins. Officials can also take this opportunity to address the players and explain the player uniform and equipment rules to them along with other rules of the sport. These pre-season meetings are beneficial for officials and are a great educational opportunity for the athletes and coaches.

One area of safety that officials sometimes overlook is examining the net cables for fraying or weakening areas when checking them for coverings. Although this is not specifically addressed in the rules it is a good idea to complete this inspection at each match you officiate at. Coaches sometimes have the players put up the nets for practice or matches and do not realize there may be problems with the cables or attachments.

The first referee's stand must be properly padded but what are often overlooked with the new equipment padding are the wheels that stick out toward the court and the back wheels. These wheels are not covered and are in an area that a player can come into contact with and be injured. Padding and covering these wheels can alleviate the possibility of injury.

If safety issues cannot be solved before the match is to begin it is extremely important for the officials to address them in the pre-match conference and establish definite non-playable areas and ground rules. Officials must enforce safety rules and guidelines at all sites. It is not acceptable to ignore a safety issue, continue play, and ask that it be resolved before the next match.

Safety is addressed in the NFHS Rules Book, Case Book, and also in the NFHS Officials Code of Ethics.

It is in everyone's best interest to identify all safety problems when inspecting the court, net supports, areas adjacent to the court, and the referee's stand to ensure these problems are taken care of prior to the match. Correct any hazardous situations as they occur. Failing to do so jeopardizes the safety of participants. If a floor becomes wet, dry it immediately with towels or mops.

Safety also applies to player equipment such as aim, knee, elbow, and ankle braces, hair devices, jewelry, body piercing and addressing glitter and body paint.

Safety issues can also arise when officials do not address sportsmanship issues immediately. This applies not only to players and coaches but also to the crowd. When problems occur with a coach, player, scorekeeper, timer or bench personnel the officials are to address the issue in an impartial controlled manner. If the problem occurs in the spectator area the officials are to ask the home administration to take care of the problem. If the home administration is not available the official will ask the home coach to resolve the problem and play will be suspended until it is resolved.

Officials must also keep in mind and follow correct procedures when dealing with blood issues on the court and on player uniforms. There is Communicable Disease and Skin Infection Procedures that official's should educate themselves with in the NFHS Rule Book.

Heat can also be a serious health issue. Officials can at any time during a set stop play and allow players to hydrate themselves when heat is an issue at the facility. Be observant and mindful of the temperature and players.

To be pro-active for player safety the officials should also make themselves aware of where the trainer is at the site to ensure immediate help is available or what procedures the coach has for injuries that occur during the match. Officials should not treat an injury or assist in removing an injured player from the court. Allow the trainer or school personnel to take care of the situation.

Accidents and injuries can occur at any time at any site and as officials, we are charged with ensuring that each site is as safe as possible and establishing ground rules for problem areas. The best practice is for officials to educate themselves in recognizing safety issues and deal with them in a firm respectful manner. Officials have a professional obligation to follow correct safety rules and guidelines throughout the match and practice good risk management at every match.

Although there are many safety issues that have not been addressed in this article the ones that I have talked about have occurred more frequently over the years. Whether it is aging equipment and facilities or officials becoming complacent due to familiarity with a site having officiated numerous times at that school, safety must remain a high priority and monitored at all times.

7

Basic Volleyball Rules, Volleyball Positions and Player Roles

---

In the game of volleyball, there are six main areas of the court occupied by players that have specific roles. There are three players in the front row of the court, and three players in the back row. These players rotate in a clockwise manner each time they win the serve. Below are explanations of the different player positions and roles on the court.

Volleyball Positions

Setter: The setter is the person that distributes the ball to the team's attackers. This person is a leader on the team, much like a quarterback on a football team, or a point guard on a basketball team. The setter has to think quickly and run plays for the offense. The setter ideally contacts every second ball when their team is receiving the serve.

Fig. Setter

Outside Hitters: There are two outside hitters on a team. Their main responsibility is to attack the ball and put it down inside the boundaries on the opponent's side of the court. These hitters attack the ball from the left of the court. They receive the majority of the sets during the game. The outside hitters usually have solid back row skills which allow them to stay in the game for all rotations.

3 Player Block

Middle Hitter: This player has excellent blocking skills. The middle hitter moves along the net and blocks the attacks from the opponent. The middle hitter attacks balls that are set quickly because of the close position to the setter in the front row. The middle hitter communicates blocking strategies to the team.

Opposite Hitter: This person hits from the right side of the court, and they are also called right side hitters. Since they are positioned in front of the opposing team's left side attackers, they must have strong blocking skills. The opposite hitter also helps the setter run the offense when the setter digs the first ball and someone else is needed to set the attackers. The opposite hitter is often one of the more versatile players on the team.

Outside Hitter

Libero: This player is a defensive specialist. The libero has strong passing and digging skills. This person plays in the back row, and they receive most of the serves from the opponent. The libero must have good ball control and communication because they start the offense for the setter and the hitters. The libero has quick reactions and they are ready to sprint, dive, and keep the ball in play for the team.

Volleyball players train hard to develop the skills needed to succeed in their designated positions. Sometimes players are capable of fulfilling multiple roles on a volleyball team. No matter how strong a player is at their certain position, the only way to win is if all players work well together. The goal of every volleyball team is to have players understand their roles on the court, and cooperate with each other to effectively execute their game plan against opponents.

VOLLEYBALL BY POSITION

Volleyball positions determine what your role is out on the court during a game. Each player has a specific job to do and each position works with the teammates to make the best play possible. Below find the role of each position defined, a list of things you should do if you're playing that position and a list of attributes you need in each spot.

Middle Blocker

A good middle can read the opponent's setter like a book and is quick enough to get from one end of the court to the other to block the ball.

The middle also hits quick sets and keeps the other team's defense off balance. A great middle blocker is a major key to your team's defense.

Outside Hitter

An outside hitter is a great all-around player. Not only does the outside need great ball-handling skills, but he needs to be a solid hitter and blocker.

Libero

The libero plays in the backrow and has impeccable ball control. The libero needs to be a great passer and an even better digger. She is all over the court to keep the ball in the air for her team to create scoring chances.

Setter

The setter is the backbone of the offense and makes the decisions about who gets the ball when. She touches the ball on the second contact and delivers it to her hitters. She needs to be able to take in a lot of information at once and to make good decisions in a split second. Consistency here is key.

Opposite

The opposite plays opposite the setter on the right front and hits sets behind and in front of the setter.

The opposite is responsible for blocking the opponent's outside hitter, which means the person who plays opposite needs to be a solid blocker as well as a good hitter. The opposite is also needed to pass and set, so should have great ball handling skills.

VOLLEYBALL: PLAYER POSITIONS

In volleyball there are 6 players on each side. Three of the players are positioned on the front court and three on the back court. Players have to rotate clockwise whenever their team wins serve so their positions on the court will change. However, their positions on the team may remain somewhat the same with a certain players always being responsible for setting, digging, or attacking. Typically players in the front row will be attackers and blockers, while players in the back row will be passers, diggers, and setters. However, these roles are not set in stone and different teams may employ different volleyball strategies.

Here is a list of typical volleyball positions and the roles they play on the team:

Setter

The setter's main job is to put the ball in the perfect place for the attackers. Typically they will take a pass from another player and take the second touch. They will try to put the ball softly in the air at just the right height for an attacker to spike the ball into the opponent's court.

The setter also runs the offense. They have to be quick both physically (to get to the ball) and also mentally (to decide where and who to set the ball to). The volleyball position setter is much like the point guard in basketball.

Middle Blocker

This volleyball position is both the main blocker and the attacker for the middle of the net. Top level teams will often have 2 players playing this position on the court at the same time.

Outside Hitter

The outside hitter is focused on the left side of the court and is generally the main attacking position. They tend to get most of the sets and most of the attacking shots in the game.

Weekside Hitter

The weekside hitter is positioned on the right side of the court. This is the backup attacker. Their primary job is blocking against the other team's outside hitter.

Liberos

The volleyball position responsible for defense is the liberos. This player will generally receive the serve or dig the attack. There are unique rules for this position as well. They wear a different color jersey from the rest of the team and they can substitute for any player on the court generally replacing a player on the back row.

Volleyball Position Skills

The hitters, attackers, and blockers are generally tall players that can jump high. They need to be able to jump above the net for spikes and blocks. Setters and liberos players need to be quick and able to pass and set the ball with a lot of control.

BASIC DESCRIPTIONS OF VOLLEYBALL POSITIONS

Rotational six positions of Volleyball

On this page we present volleyballplaying positions (libero, outside hitter etc).

If you were looking for rotational positions of volleyball (position 4, position 6 etc) and how players should line up, go to "6 positions of volleyball" page. The link is in the end of this page.

Rotational Volleyball Positions

Volleyball court divides into attack zone (front row) and defense zone (back row).

Basics of volleyball positions on the court

- There are three players on each of the zone.

- Front row players are players who are allowed to block the opponent and attack the ball in the attack zone.
- Back row players are players who play defense by digging opponent's attacks and attack the ball behind attack line (3 meter line, 10 feet line).
- Players are rotating clockwise on the court after winning the rally after the opponent's serve.

Players have rotational positions (position 5, position 2 etc.) on the court from which they are allowed to move to their playing positions (opposite, middle hitter etc.) after the serve when appropriate.

Volleyball positions on the court can also be called zones. Position 4 being called zone 4 etc.

Playing Positions in Volleyball

Volleyball positions in a team:

- Outside hitter (also called wing spiker, left side)
- Right side hitter (wing spiker, right side)
- Opposite Hitter (attacker)
- Setter
- Middle Blocker (center, middle hitter)
- Libero
- Defensive Specialist

Outside Hitter (also called wing spiker, left side)

Outside Hitter is the player who carries the serve receive responsibility along with the libero.

Outside hitter most often attacks the balls which setter sets to the antenna to the left side of the court.

Therefore after the serve outside hitters place themselves to the left front position. Sometimes setters run offensive plays in which outside hitters run to hit balls "inside" around the middle blockers.

Outside hitters play both the front row and the back row. In modern high level volleyball outside hitters are responsible for hitting the 3 meter or 10 feet line attacks, usually from the middle back position when playing in the back row.

Playing on the outside hitter's position requires great all around skills because they play through the front row and the back row.

Wing spikers have to have the skills to pass, attack, block, serve and play defense.

Wing spikers along with the opposites are often players who score the most points in the game.

Outside hitter's passing responsibility makes them extremely important player for the team.

Right side hitter (also called wing spiker)

Right side hitter has the similar role than outside hitter, they play front row and back row and are carrying pass, attack, block, serve and defense responsibilities.

Right side hitters aim to place themselves to the right front playing position.

When playing top level international volleyball on the back court right side hitters often have 3 meter or 10 feet attack responsibility from the middle back position.

Right side hitter can be also called a wing spiker.

Opposite Hitter

The opposite hitter is the player who most often scores the most points in the team.

Opposite hitters don't have the passing responsibilities. They stand behind the passers on the rotation while libero and outside hitters pass the ball and place themselves to the left front, right front or right back playing position.

The opposite usually get the most sets in the game.

Often counter attack sets after the defensive play go to the opposite hitters - they carry the responsibility of hitting the ball against a solid block when the pass is off the net.

Opposites need to have great blocking skills since they play against the opposite hitter of the opponent or opponent's outside hitter when in the front row.

Opposites also need to have defensive skills because they also play the back row where they are responsible of hitting 3 meter or 10 feet balls from the right back position.

In professional volleyball opposites along with setters have traditionally been the highest paid individuals - those are volleyball positions in most demand.

Setter

The setter is the playmaker, point guard or the quarterback of the volleyball team.

A setter's responsibility is to run the team's offense and build up offensive scoring opportunities for the team.

The setter plays both front row and back row, therefore s/he needs to be able to block, serve and play defense.

The setter needs to have good blocking skills because in front row position s/he plays against the opponent's outside hitter who often carries big load of the attacking responsibility for the team.

The setter plays the right front or the right back position

Middle Blocker (Center, Middle, Middle Hitter)

Middle blockers main responsibility is to stop the opponent's offense.

The middle blocker builds a block which stops the ball, or allows the team to dig the ball up.

Middle blockers' job is to stop the opponent's middle hitters or wing hitters in co-operation with teammates.

Middle blockers need to have great blocking, attacking and serving skills.

Middle Blockers in the Back Row

In competitive volleyball middle blockers usually play defense only on one rotation - after an own serve. After losing the rally after an own serving turn, a libero usually comes in and replaces the middle blocker. The middle blocker usually don't master in defense because they hardly play any of it. However, at junior level practicing defense and even passing is very recommended for the middles. Junior coaches should allow players to practice all the skills equally to ensure their overall skill development. This improves their athleticism and prepares players to play other positions - i.e. they may not be tall enough to play middle in the future.

Libero

The libero is fairly new position in volleyball. The libero is a back row specialist who is allowed to play back court only.

The libero wears a different color shirt in the team and is allowed to enter and exit the game without substitution request.

The libero can replace any player on the court and most often replaces middle blockers.

The libero is not allowed to serve the ball. (Some leagues in US allow liberos to serve.)

Since playing in the back court only, the libero needs to have the best passing and defensive skills in the team. The libero need to have exceptional serve receive skills because often they pass a larger area than other serve receivers in the team.

Libero most often plays the left back position.

Defensive Specialist Most leagues in United States allow unlimited substitutions; therefore very often in the team there are defensive specialists.

Defensive specialists in US enter the game to replace players who in international volleyball would be playing both the front and the back row.

Defensive specialists carry a serve receive and defense responsibility in the back row.

Defensive specialists are allowed to serve and often play the full back row rotation before giving the spot in the front row to the offensive player again.

BASIC VOLLEYBALL RULES

Volleyball is a game played by two teams on a rectangular court divided by a net. The object of the game is to send the ball over the net and ground it within the boundary lines on the opponent's side of the court. The first team to reach a certain number of points wins the game. The following overview will cover general rules that are applied in most volleyball settings.

Volleyball Rules

The Serve

The Serve: The first serve of the game is determined by a coin toss. The server must serve from behind the end line. The ball may be served underhand or overhand. The ball must be clearly visible to opponents before the serve. The ball is allowed to graze the top of the net and drop to the other side for a point.

Scoring: In rally point scoring, points can be scored by either team after every play of the ball. Points are awarded after every fault to the team that didn't commit the fault. Games are played to 21 or 25 points. A volleyball match consists of 3 games or 5 games. The first team to win 2 out of 3 games or 3 out of 5 games is the match winner. Tiebreakers are played to 15. A team must win by 2 points.

Rotation: A team will rotate each time they win the serve. Players will rotate in a clockwise manner. There will be two to six players on each side of the court.

Ball Out of Bounds

Playing the Ball: Each team is allowed to hit the ball a maximum of three times before they have to send it over the net. Most of the time, the three contacts are a pass, set, and a hit, but any combination of legal contacts is allowed. A legal contact is any contact with the ball above the waist in which the ball does not come to a rest. A player is not allowed to hit the ball twice in a row. The ball can be played off the net on the serve or during a rally. A ball is considered inbound if it hits the boundary line on the court.

Violations: A fault is called when a player steps on or over the line on a serve. Also, a service fault occurs when the ball touches a member of the serving team, lands out of bounds on the opponent's side of the net, or fails to go over the net. It is a violation to hit the ball illegally (carrying, palming, or throwing).

Players are not allowed to touch the net at anytime. Teams must serve in the correct order.

Playing Area: Both indoor and outdoor courts are approximately 18m X 9m in length. The net height for men is 2.43m and the net height for women is 2.24m.

POSITIONS IN VOLLEYBALL

USA Today Sports

There is so much more to volleyball than just rotating around the court. There are seven different positions in volleyball, and each player has a specific role to play. In order to take your understanding of the sport of volleyball to the next level, it is important to know the significance of each position.

Positions In Volleyball

Outside Hitter (aka OH, outside, pin, left side)

An outside hitter hits and blocks from the left side of the court. Normally, they also carry the responsibilities of passing and playing defense when they get to the back row. The outside typically gets the most sets, especially when the setter is out of system, due to the fact that the outside set is one of the easier options to set. An outside's responsibilities include hitting from the front and back row, passing in serve receive, playing left or middle-back defense, and blocking.

Opposite Hitter (aka OPP, pin, right side)

Opposite hitters earned that title because they are opposite to the strong (left) side hitter, meaning they hit behind the setter. In a 6-1, just like an outside hitter, an opposite has the option to play all the way around, passing, playing defense, and hitting out of the back row.

An opposite's responsibilities include swinging from the front and back row, playing right-back defense, and blocking the other team's outside hitter.

Middle Blocker (aka MB, middle hitter, middle)

Middle blockers are the team's best blockers, and they hit mostly fast-tempo sets from the middle of the court and behind the setter. Typically the libero goes in for the middle when he or she rotates to the back row. Middle sets are some of the most difficult to set and require good passes, therefore middles often get the fewest sets but have the best hitting percentages.

Setter (aka S)

A setter's primary responsibility is to take the second ball and set it up for one of the hitters to attack. Often referred to as the quarterback, the setter is the decision maker of the team and is in charge of leading the offense. In a 6-1, the setter plays all the way around, meaning that he or she has defensive responsibilities, as well as blocking duties when in the front row. A setter's responsibilities include setting the ball on the second contact to the hitters on the court, directing the offense, playing right-back defense, and blocking the other team's outside hitter.

Libero (aka L)

Liberos wear a jersey of a different color and play in the back row five out the six rotations, usually subbing in for both middle blockers. When the libero comes in for another player, it does not count as a substitution. Liberos are defensive and serve-receive specialists who are typically fast and are able to change direction quickly. Liberos are not permitted to attack the ball from above the height of the net, and they can only overhand set a front-row attacker from behind the 10-foot line.

Defensive Specialists (aka DS)

Much like a libero, a defensive specialist plays in the back row and is responsible for playing defense and receiving serve. Unlike the libero, they do not wear different colored jerseys and are required to abide by the normal substitution rules, meaning they are only in for three out of the six rotations.

Serving Specialist (aka SS)

A serving specialist is a player who subs in just to serve. These players typically have a very tough or very consistent serve, and they come in for a player who is less strong behind the service line, but otherwise very valuable to have on the court as an offensive or defensive threat.

VOLLEYBALL: STRATEGY AND TEAM PLAY

Volleyball skills and strategy go hand in hand. Developing the right skills and team strategy is key to winning matches.

The Volleyball Serve

Each point starts with a serve. Having a strong volleyball serve and service strategy can help your team greatly. How the ball is hit, where it is hit, and which player you hit it to all need to be considered.

It is important to practice your serve. Pick a style you want to master and then practice it to perfection. It helps to practice in scrimmages or under pressure as well.

Most beginners will serve the ball underhand to make sure they get the ball in play. Expert volleyball players will serve the ball overhand, however. Some players work on getting a topspin on the ball so it will dive quickly into the court. Other players will hit the ball with no spin making it float and possibly change directions in the air erratically. To get more speed and angle on the serve, some players employ a jump serve where they toss the ball in the air and jump to hit the ball at a high point.

Volleyball Passing and Setting

Passing and setting are important skills and also important in strategy.

The pass is the first hit in the sequence. It may be a bump with the forearms or a hit with the fingers. The idea is to get control of the ball. Get the ball in the air to a setter with enough control so the setter can focus on making a good set and not worry about digging or getting to the ball.

The set is the next hit in the sequence. A set is typically made with the fingertips to help control the positioning of the ball for the attack. Strategies include forward or backward setting or dumping the volleyball quickly over the net to an open spot before the opponent is ready.

Volleyball Attacking

The final shot in the sequence is the attack. The goal of the attack shot is to hit a winning ball that lands into the opponent's court.

Typically this is a spike or hard shot where the attacker jumps and hits the set ball down hard into the opponent's side. Footwork and quick steps prior to the jump can be key in hitting a winning shot. The attack doesn't have to be a spike, however. Other effective shots can be dinks, dunks, and dips where the ball is hit quickly over or around the blockers and into an open space on the court.

Volleyball Blocking

Blocking is an essential part of volleyball strategy. Players try to block the attack of the opponent and send the ball directly back into the others teams court. Deciding when to block and when to back off and try to pass and set the attack shot is key to strategy. Often teams and players will fake one and do the other to throw off the attacker.

Formations

The main differentiation in volleyball formations is in the number of setters vs. the number of attackers. There are three main formations used by most teams. They are 4-2 6-2 and 5-1. Beginners typically use a 4-2 where there are 4 attackers and 2 setters. Most advanced teams will use a 5-1 formation with a single setter and 5 attackers.

8

Basic Equipment Used in Volleyball

More than 24 million Americans and 800 million people worldwide have discovered their passion for volleyball, a sport that originated in America and is now over 117 years old and a popular Olympic event. Volleyball provides a great workout, as well as a chance to participate in a team sport. Whether you're thinking of joining a league or creating your own pick-up game, there are several key pieces of equipment that you'll need to help you slam and spike your way up to speed.

The Ball

The standard volleyball is made of leather or synthetic leather, weighs between 9 and 10 ounces and has a circumference of 25.6 to 26.4 inches. The ball has a rubber bladder and can be one color or a combination of colors. Synthetic leather is lighter and is fine for beginner players. Junior volleyballs for children 12 years old and younger weigh between 7 and 8 ounces.

The Net and Court

The outdoor volleyball court measures 18 x 9 m, surrounded by a free zone that is 2 meters wide on all sides. The minimum playing space for U.S. volleyball competitions is 7 meters. The volleyball net is 32 feet long by 3 feet wide. For women, the net should be 7 feet, 4 1/8 inches high. For men, the net should be

7 feet, 11 5/8 inches high. U.S. regulation volleyball playing surfaces must be flat and not present any hazards to the players.

Net & Poles

The net divides the volleyball court into two halves. The height of the net varies based on the age of the players and the surface being played on. An indoor net is 7 feet 11 5/8 inches in height for men and 7 feet 4 1/8 inches for women. Beach volleyball nets are hung at the same height. In addition to the nets, and the poles from which they are hung, protective padding is required to surround these structures to ensure player safety in case of collision.

Lines

The playing court is marked by two sidelines and two end lines. All lines must be 2 inches wide and must be created with a light color that is easy to discern from the playing court. An attack line should be placed three meters from the center line. The center line divides the court into two 9 x 9 meter courts.

Posts and Cables

The volleyball net structure is held together with metal cables and posts. Posts are placed 0.5 to 1.0 meter outside the sidelines and 2.55 meters high. Posts should be round, smooth and padded, to prevent injury to the players should they dive or crash into them. Metal wires and cables may need to be covered if it is determined that they present a danger to the players.

Antenna and Side Bands

Antenna are flexible rods that are 1.8 meters long made of fiberglass, fastened at the outer edge of each side band. Side bands are two white bands attached vertically to the net and placed above each sideline.

Knee pads

Knee pads should be sturdy enough to protect your knees from falls, slides and dives, but flexible enough to allow you to bend comfortably. Your volleyball knee pads must be made of fabric that breathes and manages moisture.

Good quality pads have a gel or foam shock-absorbing material that will cover and protect your patella. It is best to purchase your pads from a reliable sporting goods store that will allow you to try them on.

If you have difficulty finding the right fit, have the store professional measure you and order custom-fit pads. Popular volleyball knee pad brands include Asics, Mizuno, adidas, Nike and Mikasa.

Shoes

Arch and ankle support is key when choosing a volleyball shoe. Mizuno, Asics and Nike are just a few of the popular brands of volleyball shoes, which are lightweight, allowing you to be faster on your feet, as well as bearing good shock absorption on your toes.

Volleyball shoes also provide for better lateral movement than typical running or cross-training shoes.

Clothing and Jewelry

All clothing should be lightweight to allow maximum flexibility and breath-ability, as well as made of a material that absorbs sweat and keeps skin dry.

Spandex shorts are a good option, as they are flexible, light and absorb odor. Socks, while not required, absorb sweat and prevent blisters. Jewelry is not permitted in volleyball, with the exception of smooth wedding bands. Glasses must be worn with a strap to keep them secure.

Training for Success

Creative inventions promise to improve technique. While no one gadget can create a better player, when used in conjunction with expert coaching, training tools can be an effective way to correct flaws in the execution of many basic volleyball moves.

The "Volleyball Pass Rite System" is a simple system of rubber bands paired with wrist and ankle cuffs which restrict players arm motion to prevent over-swinging while bumping the ball. Spike trainers are used to improve the approach and execution of the spike.

Various incarnations of the spike trainer exist, though they all consist of a ball suspended from a pole secured to a base. The height of the ball is adjusted to simulate the different game-time scenarios.

VOLLEYBALL FACILITIES & EQUIPMENT

Volleyball was invented in 1895 by William G. Morgan as a less-strenuous alternative to basketball for middle-aged men. The sport began as a loose conglomeration of several other sports, incorporating equipment and ideas from badminton, tennis and basketball. As the game developed, the court and equipment used became uniquely refined to meet the specific needs of the sport.

Volleyball Equipment and Court

An indoor volleyball is typically white, but may have some other colors as well. It's round with 8 or 16 panels and is usually made of leather. The official indoor volleyball is 25.5 -26.5 inches in circumference, weighs 9.2 - 9.9 ounces, and has 4.3-4.6 psi air pressure. A youth volley ball is slightly smaller. Beach volleyballs are slightly bigger, weigh the same, but have much less air pressure.

The volleyball court is 18 meters long and 9 meters wide. It's divided in sides in the middle by the net. The net is 1 meter wide and is set up so that the top of the net is 7 feet 11 5/8 inches above the ground (right around 8 feet).

The only other key feature is a line that is drawn on each side 3 meters from the net and parallel to the net. This line is called the attack line. It defines the front row and back row areas.

History

Morgan's original game used the rubber bladder out of a basketball as the first volleyball, which was hit over a badminton net that was suspended 6 ½ feet off of the ground.

The court was divided into two 25-foot square halves, and each team was allowed to have as many players as could fit on the court.

Roughly one year after the sport was created, Spalding designed the first official volleyball, and by 1900 the ball used became more or less standardized. By 1928, the United States Volleyball Association was established to oversee the sport and ensure that standards were established for all court and equipment usage.

Court

Today, courts must meet the specifications set forth by USA Volleyball and the international governing body, FIVB. Indoor courts must measure 18 meters long by 9 meters wide and have an attack area demarcated 3 meters back from the centerline.

The lines used on the court should not be any wider than 5 cm. A free space measuring 2 meters in any direction is recommended around the playing area of the court to prevent any accidental obstructions of play. Above the highest point of the net, there should be at least 7 meters of space to allow the ball free travel, though 12 meters is recommended.

Ball

The ball used for volleyball is smaller than the basketball bladder that was used originally. For indoor volleyball, it should have a circumference between 65 and 67 cm when fully inflated to an inner pressure between 4.3 and 4.6 lbs. psi. Once inflated, the ball must weigh between 260 and 280 g. During FIVB competitions and world events, three balls are used and must meet the same standards as the other balls before being approved for play.

Net

Net height can vary depending on the age of the players and the class of volleyball being played. The standard height used for men over the age of 15 is 2.43 meters measured from the lowest point of the net to the court floor.

For women over the age of 13, the standard measurement is 2.24 meters. The net extends to each of the sidelines on the court and should be the same height at both sidelines. The net itself is 1 meter wide.

At either end of the net, an antenna is attached that is 10 mm in diameter and extends 1.8 meters above the net. These antennae are considered part of the net and are used to delineate the vertical crossing space.

Beach

The beach variant of volleyball began in the 1940s. While many of the rules and specifications of this format are the same as indoor volleyball, there are some differences. The court used in beach volleyball is slightly smaller, measuring 16 meters by 8 meters. The ball also is increased in size to a circumference between 66 and 68 cm. The average net height for men and women stays the same.

THE FACILITIES AND EQUIPMENTS USED IN PLAYING VOLLEYBALL

There are different ball games that are played today. People around the world make use of balls in different varieties of games .Among of these ball games are soccer, softball, basketball, football, volley ball and many more.

These games or sports use different methodologies, different styles and techniques, different systems, different numbers of players, different facilities as well as different equipments as well as others.

There are different ball games that are played today. People around the world make use of balls in different varieties of games .Among of these ball games are soccer, softball, basketball, football, volley ball and many more.

These games or sports use different methodologies, different styles and techniques, different systems, different numbers of players, different facilities as well as different equipments as well as others.

Even though these different ball games have different characteristics, they all share a common feature; all of these games or sports make use of ball as one of the primary equipment although these balls differ in features.

There are facility and equipments that is needed in order to play the volleyball. These are the playing courts, the net and the Volley ball.

The playing court should be a leveled area that is free from any obstruction. The court has the dimension of eighteen (18) meters by (9) nine meters. This is divided equally into two parts. There is a center line beneath the net that makes this division.

The spiking line is within three (3) meters in every side of the center line. The service area of the court is drawn outside the boundary line. It is located on the right side corner just facing the net.

The net that is use in the Volleyball game is about one (1) meters wide and (9) meters long. It has the height of two and forty three (2.43) meters for the men and two and twenty four (2.24) meters for the women.

The ball that is use in the Volleyball game has the circumference of twenty seven (27) to twenty five (25) inches for the men and twenty six (26) for the woman. The weight of the ball for the men is ten (10) to nine (9) ounces and for the women it has the weight of seven (7) ounces.

Playing Volleyball requires know-how, skills or talents. It is important for one to know at least the basics methods on how to serve a ball, on how to pass the ball to the team mates, on how to spike the ball as well as on the knowledge about the basic rules in playing the game.

The Volleyball game is not only for fun, for entertainment or for sports competition purposes. It could also be used as a way of having a physical exercise that is beneficial for an individuals' health.

POPULAR GEAR FOR COMPETITIVE VOLLEYBALL

Volleyball Knee Pads

Knee pads are an important part of the volleyball uniform. In order to play volleyball aggressively, every player needs to have the needs well protected.

Knee pads are important for making athletic defensive plays diving to the floor.

There are also many serve receive and defensive techniques that involve going to the knees. The knee pads provide added support for performing such skills as volleyball knee drops.

Volleyball Shoes

Every sport you requires the appropriate athletic shoes. And not all sports shoes are created equal. Volleyball shoes tend to lighter than baskeball shoes. Volleyball shoes also don't have a high heel lift.

Socks

Volleyball socks that wick away sweat are a must.

Low Rider Shorts

You gotta look good out there on the court. Looking like a real volleyball player is part of success.

9

Volleyball at the Summer Olympics

Volleyball has been part of the Summer Olympics program for both men and women consistently since 1964.

Brazil, United States, and the former Soviet Union, are the only teams to win multiple gold medals at the men's tournament since its introduction. The remaining five editions of the Men's Olympic Volleyball Tournament were won each by a different country including Japan, Poland, Netherlands, Russia and the defunct Yugoslavia.

Gold medals are less evenly distributed in women's volleyball than in men's; the fourteen editions of the Women's Olympic Volleyball Tournament were won by only five different countries: Brazil, Cuba, China, Japan and the former Soviet Union.

History

Origins

The history of Olympic volleyball can be traced back to the 1924 Summer Olympics in Paris, where volleyball was played as part of an American sports demonstration event. Its addition to the Olympic program, however, was given only after World War II, with the foundation of the FIVB and of some of the continental confederations. In 1957, a special tournament was held during the 53rd IOC session in Sofia, Bulgaria, to support such request. The competition was a success, and the sport was officially introduced in 1964. The Olympic Committee initially dropped volleyball for the 1968 Olympics, meeting protests. The volleyball Olympic tournament was originally a simple competition, whose format paralleled the one still employed in the World Cup: all teams played against each other team and then were ranked by number of wins, set average and point average.

One disadvantage of this round-robin system is that medal winners could be determined before the end of the games, making the audience lose interest in the outcome of the remaining matches.

To cope with this situation, the competition was split into two phases: a "final round" was introduced, consisting of quarterfinals, semifinals and finals. Since its creation in 1972, this new system has become the standard for the volleyball Olympic tournament, and is usually referred to as the "Olympic format".

The number of teams involved in the games has grown steadily since 1964. Since 1996, both men's and women's indoor events count 12 participant nations. Each of the five continental volleyball confederations has at least one affiliated national federation involved in the Olympic Games.

Men's winners

The first two editions of the volleyball Olympic tournament were won by the Soviet Union team. Bronze in 1964 and silver in 1968, Japan won gold in 1972. In 1976, the introduction of a new offensive skill, the back row attack, helped Poland win the competition over the Soviets in a very tight five-setter.

In 1980, many of the strongest teams in men's volleyball belonged to the Eastern Bloc, so the American-led boycott of the 1980 Summer Olympicsdid not have as great an effect on these events as it had on the women's.

The Soviet Union collected their third Olympic gold medal with a 3–1 victory over Bulgaria. With a Soviet-led boycott in 1984, the United States confirmed their new volleyball leadership in the Western World by sweeping smoothly over Brazil at the finals. In that edition a minor nation, Italy, won their first medal, but Italy would rise to prominence in volleyball in later decades.

A long-awaited confrontation between the US and Soviet volleyball teams came in the 1988 final: powerplayers Karch Kiraly and Steve Timmons pushed the United States to a second gold medal setting the issue in favor of the Americans.

In 1992, Brazil upset favorites Unified Team, Netherlands, and Italy for their first Olympic championship. Runners-up Netherlands, with Ron Zwerver and Olof van der Meulen, came back in the following edition for a five-set win over Italy.

In spite of their success in other major volleyball competitions in the 1990s, Italy did not fare well at the Olympics. After winning bronze in Atlanta, Serbia and Montenegro, led by Vladimir and Nikola Grbiæ, beat Russia at the final in 2000 to secure the gold (in 1996 and 2000 they played under the name Federal Republic of Yugoslavia).

In 2004, Brazil beat Italy in the final, adding a second gold medal to their record and confirming their role as the men's volleyball superpowers of the 2000s.

In 2008, United States beat Brazil in the final, winning their third gold medal. Russia won the bronze for the second time by defeating Italy. In the 2012 final, Russia came back from a 0–2 set deficit, not letting the Brazilians take advantage of any of their 2 match points in the third set. Dmitriy Muserskiy scored 31 points, which is an Olympic Games record in a final. Italy defeated Bulgaria and took Bronze.

After coming up short in the previous two editions of the Olympics as runners-up, the Brazilians captured their third gold medal in the history of the competition playing home in 2016 after their straight-set victory against Italy in the final. The United States pulled off a comeback from a 0–2 deficit to claim the bronze medal with a victory over Russia.

Gold medals appear to be more evenly distributed in men's volleyball than in women's: former Soviet Union (three titles),

United States (three) and Brazil (three) are the only teams to have won the tournament more than once. The remaining four editions were won each by a different country. Despite being a major force in men's volleyball since the 1990s, Italy are still the only volleyball powerhouses that lack a gold medal at the Olympic Games.

Women's winners

The opening edition of the volleyball Olympic tournament, in 1964, was won by the host nation Japan. There followed two victories in a row by the Soviet Union, in 1968 and 1972. South Korea were expected to get their first gold after beating Japan in the 1975 Pre-Olympic Games, but Japan came back again in 1976 for one last Olympic gold before losing their status of women's volleyball superpowers.

The American-led boycott of the 1980 Games left many strong volleyball nations like Japan and South Korea out of the games. As a result, the Soviet Union easily secured a third Olympic gold medal. In 1984, the Eastern bloc was, in its turn, boycotting the games, and the Soviet Union did not participate. As a result, host nation United States won its first medals in volleyball, losing the finals to China. With eastern and western nations again involved in the Olympics, the Soviet Union obtained a remarkable victory over Peru after trailing 0–2 in 1988's marking one of the most dramatic female matches of the 20th century. The 1988 games were, however, boycotted by Cuba.

1992 saw a new force go down in Olympic history: organized under the name Unified Team, the remnants of former Soviet Union went as far as the finals, but did not resist the power play of the young, rising Cuban squad. Led by superstars Mireya Luis and Regla Torres, Cuba would eventually set the record for consecutive wins in the Olympic Games by also taking the gold in 1996 and 2000 against China and Russia, respectively.

In 2004, the winners were once again China. Second were Russia who beat Brazil in a very tough and dramatic semifinal match after being down 1–2, 19–24 in the fourth set.

In 2008, Brazil finally won the gold, beating the United States in the final and losing only one set in the competition. China were awarded the bronze by beating Cuba. After a troubled start, Brazil secured the double gold in 2012 after beating favorites United States once again in the final. Japan won the bronze medal after defeating South Korea.

In 2016, home team Brazil were favorites to once again win the title, thus equalling Cuba's three consecutive gold medals between 1992 and 2000. After winning all of their preliminary round matches without dropping a set, the team was, however, stunned by a young Chinese squad in a tiebreaker in the quarterfinals. China went on to win the title, their third in Olympic history, by beating Serbia in four sets in the gold medal match.In the process, Lang Ping became the first person to win a gold medal as a player in Los Angeles 1984 and repeat the feat now as a coach in Rio de Janeiro. China also became the first team to win the Olympics after losing three matches in the preliminary round. The United States defeated Netherlands 3–1 to capture the bronze medal.

The fourteen editions of the women's tournament were won by only five different countries: Brazil, China, Cuba, Japan and the former Soviet Union. Despite becoming a women's volleyball powerhouse in the 21st century, United States still lack an Olympic gold.

As sporting communions go it takes some beating -- sun, sea, sand and beach volleyball on Brazil's Copacabana in an open-air, 12,000-seater arena just meters from the waves crashing onto Rio de Janeiro's golden shore.

The 2016 Olympic competition began Saturday, at a place where hundreds of people gather each day to play the sport on courts dotted along the coastline.

Brazil's passion for the sport was evident in the kilometer-plus queue to enter the arena that stretched down Avenida Atlantica.

The delay meant the temporary stadium was barely half full when Brazil's men took to the court, although it did fill out for the women's match later in the day.

Games organizers are yet to answer CNN's request for the total number of tickets sold to the event, though they did issue a statement apologizing to people who had endured the queues while insisting that issue was now in hand.

COMPETITION FORMULA

The volleyball Olympic tournament has a very stable competition formula. The following rules apply:

Qualification

- Twelve teams participate in each event.
- Host nations are always pre-qualified.
- Two teams qualify through the Men's and Women's World Cup (this number was reduced from three prior to the 2016 Summer Olympics).
- Five teams qualify as winners of continental qualification tournaments.
- The four remaining berths are decided in world qualification tournaments.

Competition format

- For the first phase, called qualification round, teams are ranked by the FIVB World Rankings and then divided in two pools of six teams using the serpentine system. The host nation is always ranked 1.
- At the qualification round, each team plays one match against all other teams in its pool. Top four teams in each pool advance, the remaining two leave the competition.
- At the second phase, usually called final round, teams play quarterfinals, semifinals and finals.
- For the final round, matches are organized according to the results obtained in the qualification round. Let the top

four teams in each pool be A1, A2, A3, A4 (group A); and B1, B2, B3, B4 (group B). Quarterfinals would then be: A1xB4; A2xB3; A3xB2; A4xB1.

- Winners of quarterfinals play semifinals as follows: (A1/B4) x (A3/B2); (A2/B3) x (A4xB1).

- At the finals, winners of semifinals play for the gold, and losers for the bronze.

- The tournament implements very tight line-up restrictions: only twelve players are allowed, and no replacement is permitted, even in case of injuries.

10

Basic Volleyball Terminology

A

Ace: A serve that results directly in a point, usually when the ball hits the floor untouched on the receiving team's side of the court.

Assist: Helping a teammate set up for a kill.

Attack: The offensive action of hitting the ball.

Attacker: Also "hitter" and "spiker." A player who attempts to hit a ball offensively with the purpose of terminating play.

Attack Block: The defensive team's attempt to block a spiked ball.

Attack Error: An attack botched in one of 5 ways: ball lands out of bounds; ball goes into net; attacker commits center line or net violation or attacker illegally contacts ball.

Attack Line: A line 3 meters/10 feet away from, and parallel to, the net. Separates the front-row players from the back-row players. A back-row player cannot legally attack the ball above the net unless he takes off from behind this line.

B

Back row/court: Space from baseline (endline) to attack line. There are 3 players whose court positions are in this area (positions 1, 6 & 5 on court)

Back Row Attack: When a back-row player takes off from

behind the attack line (10-foot/3-meter) line and attacks the ball. Various terms A-B-C-D-PIPE-BIC.

Back set: Set delivered behind the setter.

Baseline: The back boundary of the court. Also called the end line

Block: One of the 6 basic skills. A defensive play by one or more front-row players meant to intercept a spiked ball. The combination of one, 2 or 3 players jumping in front of the opposing spiker and contacting the spiked ball with the hands.

Blocking Error: Touching the net, crossing the centerline, blocking a set or serve or any other "local" violation that occurs while making a block attempt.

C

Center line: The boundary that runs under the net and divides the court into two equal halves.

Closing the block: The responsibility of the assisting blocker(s) to angle their body relative to the first blocker.

"Cover": Refers to the hitter having his/her teammates ready to retrieve rebounds from the opposing blockers.

Cross-court attack: An attack directed diagonally from the point of attack. Also called an angle hit.

Cut shot: A spike from the hitter's strong side that travels at a sharp angle across the net.

D

Deep: Refers to sending the ball away from the net, toward the baseline of the opponent's court.

Defense: One of the 6 basic skills. The key skills used to receive the opponent's attack are digging and sprawling. The dig resembles a forearm pass from a low ready position and is used more for balls that are hit near the defender. The sprawl is a result of an attempted dig for a ball hit farther away from the defender. It resembles a dive.

Dig: Passing a spiked or rapidly hit ball and low to ground. Defensive play. Slang for retrieving an attacked ball close to the floor. Statistically scored on a 3.0 point system.

Dink: A one-handed, soft hit into the opponent's court using the fingertips. Also called a tip.

Double block: Two players working in unison to intercept a ball at the net.

Double hit: Violation. Two successive hits by the same player.

Down Ball: Type of attack. "Down" refers to the blockers who neither jump, nor raise their hands above the net.

Dump: Usually performed by the setter, who delivers the ball into the opponent's court on the second contact.

F

Five-One (5-1): An offensive system that uses five hitters and one setter.

Floater: A serve with no spin so the ball follows an erratic path.

Follow: To move with and block an attacker. Athletes may change positions with another blocker in the process.

Forearm Pass: Sometimes referred to as the "pass," "bump" or "dig".

Four-Two (4-2): An offensive system using four hitters and two setters.

Free ball: Returning the ball to the opponent without the intent to get a kill. Usually a slow, arcing pass or "roll" shot rather than a spike.

Front: Position of a blocker so that she/he can block the attacker.

Front-row: Three players whose court position is in front of the attack line (3M/10 Foot), near the net. These players are in positions 2, 3 & 4 on the court.

G

Game plan: Offensive and defensive emphasis for an opponent. Usually organized for each rotation by the coaching staff.

H

Held ball: A ball that comes to rest during contact resulting in a violation.

Hit: One of the 6 basic skills. To jump and strike the ball with an overhand, forceful shot.

Hitter: Also "spiker" or "attacker." The player who is responsible for hitting the ball.

Hitting percentage: A statistic derived from total kills minus total attack errors, divided by total attempts.

J

Joust: When 2 opposing players contact the ball simultaneously above the net causing the ball to momentarily come to rest; the point is replayed if this is called by the official.

Jump serve: The server uses an approach, toss, takeoff and serves the ball with a spiking motion while in the air. There are two main types: jump float, jump spin.

K

Key player/play : To discern a team's best player or probable next play by observation of patterns or habits.

Kill: An attack that results directly in a point or sideout.

L

Libero: A player specialized in defensive skills. This player must wear a contrasting jersey color from his or her teammates and cannot block or attack the ball when it is entirely above net height. When the ball is not in play, the libero can replace any back-row player without prior notice to the officials.

Lines: The marks that serve as boundaries of a court. 2 inches (5cm) wide.

Linesman: Officials located at the corners of the court; each linesman is responsible for ruling if the ball is legally in play along the lines for which he or she is responsible. For indicating touches and play outside of the antennae on their side of net.

Lineup: Players starting rotation and, therefore, serving order. Numbered 1,2,3,4,5,6.

Line serve: A straight-ahead serve landing near the opponent's left sideline.

Line shot: A ball spiked along an opponent's sideline, closest to the hitter and outside the block.

Load: Body position for the blockers so that they are most effective.

M

Middle back: A defensive system that uses the middle back player in 6 to cover deep spikes. Also called "6 back" defense.

Middle blocker: Usually plays in the middle of the net when in the front row and moves laterally to her blocking assignments.

Middle Up: A defensive system that uses the middle-back player in 6 to cover tips or short shots along the 3 meter/10 foot line. Also called a "6 up" defense

Mintonette: The original name of the game of volleyball, created by William Morgan.

N

Net Height: Women – 7 feet, 4-1/8 inches high (2.24m),

Men – 7 feet, 11-5/8 inches high (2.43m).

O

Off-blocker: Outside blocker not included in the double block. Also called off-side blocker.

Off-Speed Shots: An attack that is intentionally slow. Ball spiked with less than maximum force but with spin. Also called "roll" shot.

Opposite: Player who plays opposite the setter in the rotation. In some systems, this player is also a setter. In other systems, this player is called a right-side.

Outside hitter: Usually plays at the ends of the net when in the front row. Also called right-side (opposite) or left side (power).

Overhand pass: A pass with both hands open that is controlled by the fingers, with the face below the ball. Both hands simultaneously contact the ball above the head and direct it to the intended target.

Overhand serve: Serving the ball and striking it with the hand above the shoulder. Float or spin.

Overlap: A violation called if a team is lined up out of rotation when the ball is served.

Overpass: A ball passed across the net.

Overset: An errant set that crosses the net without being touched by another offensive player.

P

Pass: One of the 6 basic skills. Receiving a serve or the first contact of the ball with the intent to control the ball to another player. Also called a "bump".

Pancake: One-hand floor defensive technique where the hand is extended and slid along the floor palm down while the player dives or extension rolls so the ball bounces off the back of the hand and is considered legal.

Party ball: When the ball is passed across the net in front of attack line so the front-row attacker can immediately hit the ball on the first contact.

Penetration: The blocker's ability to reach over the net above the opponent's court.

Perimeter: Backcourt defense where 4 players arrange themselves near the boundaries of the court.

Pipe: A back-row attack from the middle of the court. Position 6.

Play: An attack with a planned fake, usually including 2 or more hitter.

Q

Quick set: An extremely low vertical set used to beat the opponent's block. Can be set at any position on the net.

R

Rally scoring: Scoring method where points can be won by the serving or receiving team.

Ready position: The flexed, yet comfortable, posture a player assumes before moving to the point of contact.

Red card: Given by the official to a player or coach for flagrant misconduct resulting in a point/side out to the opponent. Results in automatic ejection and a point/side out for the opponent.

Roof: To block a spike, usually straight down for a point.

Rotation: The clockwise movement of players around the court and through the serving position following a side out. Players must retain their initial rotational order throughout the entire game, but once the ball is contacted on serve they are allowed to move anywhere.

S

Seam: The mid-point between 2 players.

Serve: One of the 6 basic skills. Used to put the ball into play. It is the only skill controlled exclusively by one player.

Set: One of the 6 basic skills. The tactical skill in which a ball is directed to a point where a player can spike it into the opponent's court. Sets can be set at different heights and different locations on the net and offensively there are names for each of these. First number is location on net and second number height of set. (Example: 13.) Sets can also be named.

Set attack: When a setter attempts to score rather than set the ball to a setter. Also called a shoot set. Setter: The second passer whose job it is to position a pass to the hitter.

Shallow: Near the net.

Shank: Severely misdirected pass.

Side out: Change of service when a serving team has failed to score a point. Occurs when the receiving team successfully puts the ball away against the serving team, or when the serving team commits an unforced error.

Six-pack: Being hit in the face with the ball.

Six-two (6-2): An offense with four spikers and two spiker/setters. Setter comes from the back row.

Slide/step: A quick attack behind the setter.

Spike: Also called a hit or attack. A ball contacted with force by a player on the offensive team who intends to terminate the ball on the opponent's floor or off the opponent's blocker.

Split block: A double-block that leaves a space between the blockers.

Stuff: A ball deflected back to the attacking team's floor by the opponent's blockers.

Substitution: Allows one player to replace another player already on the court. Rules dictate number of subs each team is allowed.

Switch: To change court positions after a ball is served to facilitate strongest player positions.

T

Tandem: A combination in which one player attacks immediately behind another.

Tape: The top of the net.

Telegraph: To show one's intention to the opponents.

Three-meter line: The line extended across the court to signify the point which a back-row player must leave the ground behind to attack the ball. Also call "attack line" and 10-foot line

Tip: A one-handed, soft hit into the opponent's court using the fingertips. Also called a dink.

Tool: When an attacker hits the ball off an opposing blocker's arms out of bounds. Also called a wipe.

Touch: A player contacting the ball on the defensive play.

Transition: To switch from offense to defense and vice versa.

Triple-block: Block formed by all 3 front-row players.

U

Underhand serve: A serve performed with an underhand striking action. The ball is usually contacted with the heel of the hand.

W

W serve-receive formation: Three players in the front row, two in the back.

Wipe: To deliberately spike the ball off an opponent's hands and out of bounds. Also called a tool.

Y

Yellow Card: Given by the official to a player or coach as a warning of misconduct. Two yellow cards result in an automatic red card.

Bibliography

Ashok Kumar Rawat: *Coaching in Sports*, Sports Pub, Delhi, 2009.

Baitsch, H.: *The Scientific View of Sport*. New York: Springer-Verlag, 1972.

Baschke, Wendy J.: *The Archaeology of the Olympics*. Madison, Wisc.: University of Wisconsin Press, 1988.

Bhardwaj, Ramesh : *The Coach and Sports Management*, Sports Publication, Delhi, 2011.

Chakraborty, Samiran : *Fundamental of Sports Management*, Prerna Prakashan, Delhi, 2007.

Cooper, Chris: *Commonwealth Games and Tourism*, The, London, Heinemann, 1987.

Crotty, M.: *The Foundations of Social Research: Meaning and Perspective in the Research Process*. London: Sage, 1998.

Digumarti Bhaskara Rao: *Sports Management*, APH, Delhi, 2003.

Ehrlich, Matthew C.: *Sports in the Movies*. Urbana: University of Illinois Press, 2004.

Elliott, James: *Sports: Politics and Public Sector Management*, London, Retailed, 1997.

Gay L. R.: *Educational Research Competencies for Analyses and Application*. Ohio: Charles E. Merill, 1976.

Guttman, A.: *Sports Spectators*. New York: Columbia University Press, 1986.

Hall, C Michael *Sports Planning: Policies, Processes and relationships*, Harlow, Prentice Hall, 2000.

Jennings, Gayle: *Sports Economics: Research and Development*, Chichester, Wiley, 2001.

Kolah, A.: *Maximizing the Value of Sponsorship*. London: Sports Business Croup, 2003.

Lieberman, L. : *'Games and Activities for Individuals with Sensory Impairments', in Grosse,* Reston, VA, AAHPERD Publications, 1993.

Manoj Thomas: *New Era of Sports Management*, Khel Sahitya Kendra, Delhi, 2007.

Murthy, J. Krishna : *Administration and Organisation of Physical Education and Sports*, Commonwealth, Delhi, 2005.

Nafziger, JAR, *International Sports Law*, 1988, New York: Transnational

Portwood, M. : *Dyslexia and Physical Education*, London, David Fulton Publishers, 2003.

Ramesh Bhardwaj: *The Coach and Sports Management*, Sports Publication, Delhi, 2011.

Rao, Bhaskara : *Sports Management*, APH, Delhi, 2003.

Rawat, Kumar : *Coaching in Sports*, Sports Pub, Delhi, 2009.

Samiran Chakraborty: *Fundamental of Sports Management*, Prerna Prakashan, Delhi, 2007.

Schatzman, L. &. Strauss, A. L.: *Field Research: Strategies for a Natural Sociology*. Englewood Cliffs, NJ: Prentice-Hall Inc, 1973.

Shepard, R.J. : *Fitness in Special Populations*, Champaign, IL, Human Kinetics, 1990.

Simon, RL, *Fair Play: Sports, Values, and Society*, Boulder: Westview, 1991

Tourist Board: *Visitor Attractions: A Development Guide*, Edinburgh, Scottish Tourist Board, 1991.

Vanden Auweele : *Sport and Development*, LannooCampus, 2006.

Verma, J. : *A Text Book on Sports Statistics and Management*, Sports Pub, Delhi, 2009.

Winnick, J.P. : *Adapted Physical Education and Sport*, Champaign, IL, Human Kinetics, 1990.

Yesalis, C : *Anabolic Steroids in Sport and Exercise*, Champaign, Ill: Human Kinetics, 1993

Index

CPSIA information can be obtained
at www.ICGtesting.com
Printed in the USA
LVHW092139100219
607078LV00001B/280/P

9 789352 976911